THE INFILTRATION OF THE NEW AGE

THE
INFILTRATION
OF THE
NEW AGE

J. YUTAKA AMANO
NORMAN L. GEISLER

Tyndale House
Publishers, Inc.
Wheaton, Illinois

Unless otherwise noted, Scripture quotations are
from the *New American Standard Bible,* copyright
1960, 1962, 1963, 1971, 1973 The Lockman
Foundation.
Library of Congress Catalog Card
Number 88-50245
ISBN 0-8423-1606-X
Printed in the United States of America
95   94   93   92   91   90
12 11 10 9 8 7 6 5 4 3 2

CONTENTS

ONE
IS THE WEST STILL THE WEST?
The Invasion of Eastern Thought

Clouds of mist and fog weave their way through a dew-drenched forest. Amidst the luminescent aura, a young disciple listens eagerly to his wise master.

"Size has no meaning. It matters not. Look at me. Judge me by my size, do you?"

The chastened disciple denies the accusation in shame.

"And well you shouldn't," scolds his aging mentor, "for my ally is the Force. And a powerful ally it is. Life creates it and makes it grow. Its energy surrounds us and binds us. Luminous beings are we, not this crude matter."

Yoda, mentor of many would-be Jedi knights over the centuries, could see that his pupil was more confused than ever. Sweeping the air in a grand motion, Yoda continued, "You must feel the Force around you. Here, between you and me. Between the rock and . . . everywhere. Yes, even the land."

This scene is from *The Empire Strikes Back,* second part of the record-breaking *Star Wars* film trilogy. The worldview that originated in the lands of the East was echoed on the fictional swampy planet of Dagobah. *Time* magazine writer Gerald Clarke wrote of the Eastern occultism which producer George Lucas expressed so vividly in his *Star Wars* creation:

Like Yoda, Lucas is a devout believer in the Force. Says Lucas: "When you are born, you have an energy field around you. You could call it an aura. . . . It is an idea that has gone all the way through history. When you die, your energy field joins all other energy fields in the universe, and while you're still living that larger energy field is sympathetic to your own energy field."[1]

Eastern religions like Hinduism have taught for centuries that God is an impersonal energy force which, like a cosmic sponge, swallows up all distinctions and all opposites. In the Eastern worldview, God is both good and evil, love and hate. Like the Hindu concept of Brahman, "the Force has two sides." George Lucas explains:

It has a bad side to it, involving hate and fear, and it has a good side, involving love, charity, fairness, and hope. If you use it well, you can see the future and the past. You can sort of read minds and you can levitate and use that whole netherworld of psychic energy.[2]

No surprise then, that the director of *The Empire Strikes Back*, practicing Zen Buddhist Irvin Kershner, made his religious intent in the movie very explicit:

I wanna introduce some Zen here because I don't want the kids to walk away just feeling that everything is shoot-em-up, but that there's also a little something to think about here in terms of yourself and your surroundings.[3]

The *Star Wars* parallel with Eastern religion is further exemplified by its producer's belief that "when people die, their life spirit is drained from them and incorporated in a huge energy force,"[4] joining "the ethereal oneness of the Force."[5] Once again, the cosmic sponge of Hinduism makes its presence known on America's screens.

People can croak, "Entertainment! Entertainment!" until they're blue in the face. The fact remains that films like . . . Star Wars have become jerry-built substitutes for the great myths and rituals of belief, hope and redemption that cultures used to shape before mass secular society took over.[6]

George Lucas's *Star Wars* trilogy is just one of many avenues where Eastern thought has invaded pop culture. Other movies, such as *Poltergeist, Indiana Jones and the Temple of Doom, The Dark Crystal,* and *Solarbabies* have all brought an Eastern world to the movie theater.

A television show "Sidekicks" is about a Caucasian cop who takes charge of a young Asian orphan. Young Ernie proves to be a miniature Bruce Lee, with lethal kicks dispensing his enemies effortlessly. But skill and hard work are not enough to make prime-time television. ABC has thus endowed their midget martial arts expert with the habit of conversing with his deceased grandfather. And Ernie is able to get in touch with the power of the universe in order to energize his fighting skills, an ability evidenced by a mystical glow on his forehead.

On cable TV's Home Box Office, Muppet master Jim Henson's "Fraggle Rock" has presented episodes where Zen philosophy is prominent. One episode introduced a Muppet reminiscent of the David Carradine character in the popular "Kung Fu" television series of the seventies. This flute-carrying Muppet enjoins the Fraggles to "find their own song" and thus realize perfect harmony with all things. One particular frazzled Fraggle finds great difficulty in being able to intuitively discover her special song. She must finally relinquish her rational sensibilities to find her song and, ultimately, to feel the oneness of all things.

On January 18–19, 1987, actress Shirley MacLaine aired her ABC five-hour mini-series "Out on a Limb," based on her best-selling book of the same title. The book and mini-series outlined MacLaine's alleged reincarnation experiences. Her sequels *Dancing in the Light* and *It's All in the Playing,* which explore in greater detail her occult adventures, have also topped the best-seller lists. Although MacLaine insists that she is not leaving the theatrical limelight, she became more active at promoting her Eastern occultism through seminars and speaking engagements after the television debut.

In the music world, ex-Beatle George Harrison frankly disclosed his purpose behind the top-selling record "My Sweet Lord." He admitted that he wanted "to sneak up on [the audience] a bit" by gradually changing the background chant of "Hallelujah" to "Hare Krishna." After awhile, Harrison claims, they're lulled "into a sense of false security" until they're singing Hare Krishna "before they know what's happened."[7]

Singer Tina Turner attributes her career triumphs to the unleashing of her "spiritual power." Chanting *nam-myoho-renge-kyo* ("glory to the lotus sutra of the mystical law") twice a day before her altar, Turner is an avid follower of Nichiren Shoshu Buddhism.[8] This recent development (late 1200s) of ancient Buddhism predicts that world peace and unity will be attained through chanting to the Gohonzon (the sacred scroll contained in the butsodon, a black box that sits on the altar). Faithful chanting is said to tune one in to the frequencies of the universe, thereby merging one's self with the Buddha essence. Turner and Harrison are only two performers among the many who practice Eastern religions.

Many Christians may be alarmed at the "New Age" labels they find in record stores. New Age music is now a multi-million dollar sector of the recording industry despite little radio play or advertising. New Age music is hard to define even by its most dedicated fans. Referred to as "high tech Muzak" by some, this highly evocative blend of Oriental and Occidental music combines organic sounds (e.g., waterfalls, whale voices) with classical, jazz, and pop-rock. New Age music is meditative, "kick back" music. And while there is nothing inherently Eastern about New Age music, many of the artists are often given to statements about life that are mystical in nature.[9]

Eastern thought has also invaded far more than just popular culture. Even the sciences have not been immune to the spread of Eastern philosophies. Fritjof Capra wrote *The Tao of Physics: An Exploration of the Parallels Between Modern Physics and Eastern Mysticism* to present his claim that "the two foundations of twentieth-century physics — quantum theory and relativity theory — both force us to see the world very much in the way a Hindu, Buddhist, or Taoist sees it."[10]

Gary Zukav tries to demonstrate the parallels between the Hindu picture of Lord Krishna — "dancing with all the souls of the world" — and modern physics in his book *The Dancing of the Wu Li Masters: An Overview of the New Physics*. According to Zukav, the "recurrent theme of Eastern literature" is that "to dance with god . . . is to dance with ourselves. He goes on to say that "this is also the direction toward which the new physics, quantum mechanics, and relativity, seem to point."[11] In *Mysticism and the New Physics: A Different Way of Understanding*, author Michael Talbot promises to "explore the infinite mysteries of the universe through the age-old wisdom of the East; [and to] explore the occult phenomena which can now be explained."[12] Our educational system and business sector are now experiencing a surge of New Age thought. These areas will be discussed in subsequent chapters.

While science begins to show the infiltration of Eastern thought, it is still popular culture that is the best indicator of how Eastern thought is being accepted by the person on the street. Take, for example, an area considered to be the lowest common denominator in culture: comic books. The popular comic book, "Doctor Strange, Master of the Mystic Arts" (i.e., the occult), which even had a TV-movie debut like The Incredible Hulk, Spiderman, and Wonder Woman did, dealt with a reincarnation problem in the August 1984 issue. In this story, three monks from the Far East ask Dr. Strange to help them find their High Lama's reincarnated self. Every High Lama of Tibetan Buddhists is believed to be the same sacred soul reincarnated in a new body. But the ascetic order cannot find their reincarnated mentor in their native land. Surviving without spiritual leadership for a quarter of a century, three monks are sent to America to seek the help of Dr. Strange.

To the surprise of Dr. Strange and the displeasure of Danu, one of the monks, a blonde-haired, blue-eyed American, has been housing the spirit of his High Lama, "exposing it to the decadence of the material world." Danu therefore attempts to correct what he perceives as "a single error of reincarnation" by killing the American. "Your body must die," insists Danu, "that the Lama may be born again, purging this horrible experience from his karma." After being rescued, the Caucasian Lama then explains to his misguided disciple: "My incarnation here was not some mystical mistake. . . . So much has happened to the world in this century . . . East and West grow closer every day. It was necessary that I be reborn in America."

Whether the editors of Marvel Comics realized it or not, they stumbled upon one of the most significant ideological movements in our nation today. The West is, as Harvard Divinity School professor Harvey Cox titled his book, *Turning East*. In this work, Professor Cox writes,

> *The influence of Oriental spirituality in the West is hardly something new. But there is something new about the present situation. In previous decades, interest in Oriental philosophy was confined mostly to intellectuals and was centered largely on ideas, not on devotional practices. . . . Today, on the other hand, not only are large numbers of people who are in no sense "intellectuals" involved, but they appear more interested in actual religious practices than in doctrinal ideas. The recent wave of spirituality seems both broader and deeper than the ones that preceded it.* [13]

The fact is that large numbers of people are involved, not just a fringe group, and the extent of the interest has no precedent in American religious history. [14]

Os Guinness, friend and colleague of the late Francis Schaeffer, wrote in his widely read work, *The Dust of Death*,

> *The point is this: The East is still the East, but the West is no longer the West. Western answers no longer seem to fit the questions. With Christian culture disintegrating and humanism failing to provide an alternative, many are searching the ancient East.* [15]

Even social forecaster John Naisbitt, in his best-seller *Megatrends*, noted "the widespread interest in Eastern religions" since the 1960s. [16]

Such a widespread network of Eastern-oriented groups make up what is called the "New Age movement." Marilyn Ferguson, one of the leading promoters of the New Age movement, writes in her book *The Aquarian Conspiracy*,

> *A leaderless but powerful network is working to bring about radical change in the United States. . . . Broader than reform, deeper than revolution, this benign conspiracy for a new human agenda has triggered the most rapid cultural realignment in history. The great shuddering, irrevocable shift overtaking us is . . . a new mind—the ascendance of a startling worldview.* [17]

Ferguson believes that the "old" worldview of the Judeo-Christian heritage is decaying before our very eyes, and its funeral service is about to begin. The "new" worldview, often called the New Age movement, will rise from the ashes of its predecessor like the Phoenix of ancient times.

What exactly is this New Age movement? What do they believe? How are they organized? How do they feel about Christians and the Bible? What do they intend to accomplish, and how successful have they been so far? Is there a New Age conspiracy underway? These questions and more will be answered throughout this book.

Notes

1. Gerald Clarke, "The Empire Strikes Back!" *Time,* 19 May 1980, 73.
2. Ibid.
3. *Rolling Stone*, 24 July 1980, 37.
4. Dale Pollock, *Skywalking: The Life and Films of George Lucas* (New York: Harmony, 1983), 140.

5. James Kahn, *Return of the Jedi* (New York: Ballantine, 1983), 204.

6. *Newsweek,* 1 January 1979, 50.

7. *Update,* December 1983, 23.

8. Nancy Griffin, "Tina: The Scorching Ms. Turner Chills Out at Home," *Life,* August 1985, 25.

9. Some of the leading New Age artists are William Ackerman, Steven Halpern, Kitaro, Chaitnaya Hari Deuter, Andreas Vollenweider, Vangelis, Jean-Michel Jarre, Paul Winter, Gheorge Zamfir, Tangerine Dream, Isao Tomita, Eddie Jobson, and Lucia Hwong. However, not all musicians listed under this category accept the "New Age" label. Andreas Vollenweider is a case in point. See Bill Barol, Mark D. Uehling, and George Raine, "Muzak for a New Age," *Newsweek,* 13 May 1985, 68; Michael Walsh, "New Age Comes of Age," *Time,* 1 September 1986, 82-83; Lou Fournier, "New Age Is in Tune with the '80s," *Insight,* 30 June 1986, 56-57.

10. Fritjof Capra, *The Tao of Physics: An Exploration of the Parallels Between Modern Physics and Eastern Mysticism* (Boulder, Colo.: Shambala, 1975), 4-5.

11. Gary Zukav, *The Dancing of the Wu Li Masters: An Overview of the New Physics* (New York: Bantam, 1979), 91.

12. See the back cover of *Mysticism and the New Physics: A Different Way of Understanding* by Michael Talbot (New York: Bantam, 1981).

13. Harvey Cox, *Turning East* (New York: Simon and Schuster, 1977), 9.

14. Ibid., 92.

15. Os Guinness, *The Dust of Death* (Downers Grove, Ill.: InterVarsity, 1973), 195.

16. John Naisbitt, *Megatrends* (New York: Warner, 1982), 240.

17. Marilyn Ferguson, *The Aquarian Conspiracy* (Los Angeles, Calif.: J. P. Tarcher, 1980), 23.

TWO
THE GOD WHO IS US?
A Look at Pantheism

Depressed? Angry? Down on life? Need a job? Need love and companionship? Then you need to come on down to the God-mart. The God-mart will solve all your problems by finding the right religion for you. We've got all kinds of gods here, available in all sizes, shapes, and styles.

Welcome to the God-mart. We've got the God of deism. A great deal — all the power and wonder of the Christian God without the worry that he'll intervene and mess up your life.

We've got the gods of polytheism — a whole slew of 'em! Greek gods, Norse gods, Mormon gods, Hindu gods. Gods with wings and feathers. Gods with bodies of lions, faces of birds, and gods that are into populating other planets but don't drink coffee, tea, or Coke.

Now if you're really in fashion, you'll just love our God of pantheism. It is the God that is everywhere because it is everything. Doesn't take up shelf space because . . . well, it *is* the shelf . . . and everything else to boot. The pantheistic God never needs to be told about you or your needs because, you see, it is you.

The God-mart can take care of all your religious needs. What about truth, you say? Look, here we only sell religion, we don't sell truth. What about Christianity you ask? Listen, this is a business like any other business. We can get you New Age/Old Age pantheism, but we can't sell what's not for sale. Some teacher from Nazareth and His followers are running around giving it away free. Imagine that.

PANTHEISM: WORLDVIEW OF THE NEW AGE MOVEMENT[1]

The New Age movement came in and purchased non-exclusive rights to the pantheistic God sometime ago.[2] Listen to these statements by New Age leaders.

New Age spokeswoman Marilyn Ferguson says,

> *The separate self is an illusion. . . . The self is a field within larger fields. When the self joins the Self, there is power. . . . Even beyond the collective Self, the awareness of one's linkage with others, there is a transcendent, universal Self.[3]*

"When we're in the spiritual state," wrote New Age political activist Mark Satin, "everything merges into one great unity: the unity of the cosmos."[4] New Age prophet David Spangler received this "revelation" from the pantheistic God of the New Age: "I AM now the Life of a new heaven and a new earth. Others must draw upon Me and unite with Me to build its forms. . . . There is always only what I AM."[5]

Now while New Agers have been getting attention with the God of pantheism, the pantheistic God is a hardly a new and untested model. The New Agers' god is the long-worshiped pantheistic God of the East. The Hindus call him "Brahman" or the Absolute.[6] The Buddhist often refers to the Buddha as "the universal mind."[7]

Oddly enough, the New Age movement is really an Old Age rehash. Pantheism has always been very popular, from the "all-pervasive spirit" of savage tribes to the present-day pantheism popularized in the best-sellers of Shirley MacLaine. C. S. Lewis, who was by no means fond of pantheism, talked about man's ancient tendency to embrace pantheism:

> *Far from being the final religious refinement, Pantheism is in fact the permanent natural bent of the human mind; the permanent ordinary level below which man sometimes sinks, under the influence of priestcraft and superstition, but above which his own unaided efforts can never raise him for very long. . . . Yet, by a strange irony, each new relapse into this immemorial "religion" is hailed as the last word in novelty and emancipation.[8]*

Pantheism is the belief that God is everything and everything is God. This ancient belief has been embraced by proponents of the so-called New Age movement. New Ager Shirley MacLaine recalls her spiritual experience in the mineral baths of the Andes: "Slowly, slowly, I became the water. . . . I was the air, the water, the darkness, the walls, the bubbles, the candle, the wet rocks under the water, and even the sound of the rushing river outside."[9]

When MacLaine performs onstage, she forgets her individuality and becomes "one with the music, the lights, and the collective spirit of the audience." She says, "You are part of the audience. They are a part of you."[10] This is the all-embracing, all-enveloping belief of pantheism.

According to MacLaine, everyone and perhaps everything has a "higher self." The higher self is defined as one's "eternal unlimited soul." It is the repository of past life experiences and the link between a person's consciousness and the God-Force.[11]

Each higher self of each being is in touch with the other beings' higher selves, and these form a collective energy field. When MacLaine asked her higher self how it differed from God, it replied that there was no difference: "I am God, because all energy is plugged into the same source. We are all individualized reflections of the God source. God is us and we are God."[12]

Obviously, this means that she is God. If everything is God, and I'm a thing, then I'm God. MacLaine's higher self told her, "Each soul is its own God. You must never worship anyone or anything other than self. For *you* are God. To love self is to love God."[13]

ARGUMENTS AGAINST PANTHEISM

Contrary to Common Sense. If pantheism is true, then all is one. There is no diversity or individuality in the world. But if all is one, then there is no difference between myself and anything else. And if there is no difference between myself and anything else, then I should not call myself "myself." For to call myself "myself" is to assume that there is a difference between myself and anything else.

However, to say that I should not call myself "myself" is to deny that "myself" exists. In other words, if pantheism is true, then the self I experience does not exist.

Every time I run away from myself, there is a self to run away from. Common sense tells me that I am different from others. When I speak to my neighbor, I am not speaking to myself. And as we said before, the reality of "myself" implies that there is a difference between myself and anyone or anything else. In short, the world is filled with different people and things. Unless my senses are totally deceiving me, other persons and things do exist. I am not them. But if I am not other things, then I am not all that is. I am not God. Thus pantheism is wrong.

Another argument against the New Age God is the belief in man's evolutionary godhood. The next step in man's evolution will not be physical, but spiritual. He will realize that he is God. This is why Shirley MacLaine believes that she is God. She views her spiritual pilgrimage as an evolution into godhood.

According to one New Age author, the figure Lord Maitreya, who is considered by some to be the New Age Christ, said, "My purpose is to show man that he need fear no more, that all of Light and Truth rests within his heart, that when this simple fact is known man will become God." [14]

But if all humans are divine, then why do we act so human? This is where New Agers are forced to resort to a kind of "divine amnesia" for an explanation. "The tragedy of the human race," says MacLaine, "was that we had forgotten we were each Divine." [15]

Salvation for the New Ager is thus a kind of "I could have had a V-8" kind of theology. We go through life, needing to grasp that "I could have had my divinity realized."

New Agers look in the mirror and see a budding god. But there's one problem. God cannot bud. He cannot blossom. God has always been in full bloom. That is, God is and always has been God. He — or It — is perfect and unlimited, as even New Agers contend.

You see, New Agers hold to two contrary beliefs.

> *God is the Absolute, the Infinite, the Unlimited. We must be "enlightened" and realize our divinity.*

But one cannot be both unlimited and yet unenlightened. For to become enlightened, as all thoroughgoing New Agers have, means that you were once unenlightened. But if there was ever a time when I was not enlightened, then I cannot be God, since God has always been enlightened.

MacLaine once tried to convince a friend that he was God too. "Just listen to your feelings and trust them," she told him. "You are unlimited. You just don't realize it." [16] Well, if he's "unlimited," then why was he so limited that he did not realize he was unlimited?

Common sense demands that New Agers cannot be unlimited and enlightened. All New Agers admit that there was a time when they were not New Agers. That means, according to their own system, that there was a time when they did not know the "truth." Their perception of reality was limited, at least before they attained a kind of enlightenment. An unlimited being would not have divine amnesia.

In other words, the New Age belief in evolutionary godhood is false simply because a god cannot evolve. If there is an eternal God, then it was always "enlightened" to its own godhood.

The Real Distinction Between Good and Evil. With pantheism, all distinctions merge into a fog of one. How then does the pantheist handle the distinction between good and evil, right and wrong?

New Ager Shirley MacLaine's higher self told her that such pantheistic beliefs were meant "to eventually eliminate the artificial concepts of good and evil."[17] For the pantheist, good and evil are false categories. "There is no such thing as evil or good. There is only enlightened awareness or ignorance."[18]

In other words, "there is no evil—only the lack of knowledge."[19] The "knowledge" that we are God. One of MacLaine's spirit guides said that "the struggle back toward original divinity is what your Bible terms Satan. . . . What you term as Satan is merely the force of your lower consciousness as you engage in your struggle to return and know God, which was your origin."[20] What we call evil "is really only the lack of consciousness of God."[21]

According to this New Age ghost, "Until mankind realizes there is, in truth, no good and there is, in truth, no evil—there will be no peace."[22] Pantheists must claim that ultimately good and evil are illusory. For if God is all, then good and evil must be explained in one of the following ways:

1. God is all-good, but not evil.
2. God is all-evil, but not good.
3. God is all-good and all-evil.
4. God is only partly good and partly evil.
5. God is all and the categories of good and evil are illusory.

Option 1 cannot be true, since it would mean that evil exists apart from God. And in the pantheist system, good cannot exist apart from God because nothing exists outside of God. In other words, if Option 1 were true, then God would not be All.

For the same reason, Option 2 cannot be true either. The pantheistic God cannot be all-evil to the exclusion of good without sacrificing its all-pervasiveness.

And yet God cannot be both all-good and all-evil (Option 3), for if God is all of one thing then there is no "room" for anything else. If God is all-good, then there is no "room" for any evil.

Neither can God be only partly good and partly evil (Option 4), because this would suggest that there would exist other good and other evil outside of God. But such a scenario would be impossible in a pantheistic universe. This leaves only one alternative left: the categories of good and evil are illusory (Option 5).[23]

When Francis Schaeffer spoke to a group of students at Cambridge University, there was a Hindu who began criticizing Christianity. Schaeffer said, "Am I not correct in saying that on the basis of your system, cruelty and noncruelty are ultimately equal, that there is no intrinsic difference between them?" The Hindu agreed. One of the students immediately caught on to what Schaeffer was driving at. He picked up a kettle of boiling water that he was going to use to make tea and held the steaming pot over the Indian's head. This young Hindu looked up and asked the student what he was doing. The student said with a cold yet gentle finality, " 'There is no difference between cruelty and noncruelty.' Thereupon the Hindu walked out into the night."[24]

Ex-guru Rabindranath Maharaj came to the realization that pantheism itself could not escape the categories of good and evil:

> If there was only One Reality, then Brahman [the pantheistic god] was evil as well as good, death as well as life, hatred as well as love. That made everything meaningless, life an absurdity. It was not easy to maintain both one's sanity and the view that good and evil, love and hate, life and death were One Reality. Furthermore, if good and evil were the same, then all karma was the same and nothing mattered, so why be religious?[25]

Any notion of what is right and wrong—whether it be called morality, standards, values, or karma—is meaningless if all is one. Treating the categories of good and evil as illusions is not only unlivable, but contrary to common sense as well. Thus, "the ship of pantheism is wrecked on the reef of evil."[26]

Contrary to Scripture. Pantheists often quote Scripture as proof that Christians should hop on the Eastern bandwagon. Let's take a look at the major passages used by pantheists:

> *For this cause therefore the Jews were seeking all the more to kill Him, because He not only was breaking the Sabbath, but also was calling God His own Father, making Himself equal with God. (John 5:18)*

We admit that this verse confirms that Jesus was in fact claiming to be God. He did not deny the charges even though He spoke to Jews who believed it was blasphemy for a man to claim to be God (John 10:33). True, Jesus claimed to be the unique Son of God. However, this passage says nothing in regard to other human beings being equal with God, much less being God.

> *And so they were saying to Him, "Where is Your Father?" Jesus answered, "You know neither Me, nor My Father; if you knew Me, you would know My Father also." (John 8:19)*

Here again, this passage demonstrates the deity and distinct personalities of the Father and Son. The Father is the one who sends, and Jesus is the one sent (vv. 16, 18). In any case, this verse says nothing of pantheism. It points to theistic trinitarianism, that is, to the teaching that there is one God revealed in three distinct persons.

> *The Jews answered Him, "For a good work we do not stone You, but for blasphemy; and because You, being a man, make Yourself out to be God." Jesus answered them, "Has it not been written in your Law, 'I said, you are gods'? If He called them gods, to whom the word of God came (and Scripture cannot be broken), do you say of Him, whom the Father sanctified and sent into the world, 'You are blaspheming,' because I said, 'I am the Son of God'? If I do not do the works of My Father, do not believe Me; but if I do them, though you do not believe Me, believe the works, that you may know and understand that the Father is in Me, and I in the Father." (John 10:33-38)*

Looking at this passage through Eastern glasses, one might claim that Jesus is saying that we are all divine beings. But when Jesus answers, "Has it not been written in your Law, 'I said, you are gods'?" He is quoting Psalm 82:6. In this context, God is portrayed as the ultimate Judge (vv. 1, 8). Human judges were viewed as the manifestors of God's will and were sometimes referred to as *Elohim,* translated, "gods" or "judges." Note also that Jesus uses the term "gods" to refer not to all men but only to those "to whom the word of God came." This fits with its usage in Psalm 82 as well. The Lord God uses the term "gods" sarcastically to condemn these wicked men to whom a great honor and responsibility were entrusted. They were to be righteous judges like the True Judge, but instead corrupted their practice.

Pantheism is not being referred to here. Throughout John, Jesus is emphatically described as the unique Son of God sent by the Father (4:34; 5:23-24, 30; 6:38-40, 44, 57; 7:16, 18; 8:16, 18; 9:4; 10:36; 11:42; 12:45, 49; 14:24; 15:21; 16:5; 17:3, 18, 21, 23, 25; 20:21). The relationship between Jesus the Son and God the Father is eternal, but all believers become children of God. And there is a big difference between the eternal relationship Jesus has with God the Father and the one that believers have graciously been given. Bible scholar Gleason Archer explains this difference:

> *He is the Son of God by virtue of His innate status as God; believers are sons of God only by the gracious calling of God and by His act of adoption. By no means, then, does our Lord imply here that we are sons of God just as He is — except for a lower level of holiness and virtue. No misunderstanding could be more wrongheaded than that. But what He does affirm here is that His hearers should not be shocked at His imputing deity to Himself, when even their own Holy Scriptures accord them the status of divinity by the adoption of grace.* [27]

Consider another passage concerned with Jesus the Son of God:

> *Philip said to Him, "Lord, show us the Father, and it is enough for us." Jesus said to him, "Have I been so long with you, and yet you have not come to know Me, Philip? He who has seen Me has seen the Father; how do you say, 'Show us the Father'? Do you not believe that I am in the Father, and the Father is in Me? The words that I say to you I do not speak on My own initiative, but the Father abiding in Me does His works. Believe Me that I am in the Father and the Father in Me; otherwise believe on account of the works themselves." (John 14:8-11)*

22

Again, this verse says nothing of anyone other than Jesus being divine. The "in me / in Him, abiding" references are defined in John 15:1-10 (especially vv. 9-10) as meaning the believer should remain in the will and purpose of God. To be in Jesus, to abide in Him, is to obey His commandments. We abide in His "word" (v. 7) and His "love" (v. 9) by keeping His commandments (v. 10).

> *I do not ask in behalf of these alone, but for those also who believe in Me through their word; that they may all be one; even as Thou, Father, art in Me, and I in Thee, that they also may be in Us; that the world may believe that Thou didst send Me. And the glory which Thou hast given Me I have given to them; that they may be one, just as We are one; I in them, and Thou in Me, that they may be perfected in unity, that the world may know that Thou didst send Me, and didst love them, even as Thou didst love Me. (John 17:20-23)*

What does Jesus mean by "one"-ness? The disciples are to be "one" in the same particular sense that the Son and Father are one as described in this context. This sense is spelled out as follows:
- One is sent, the other sends (vv. 3, 8, 18, 21, 23).
- One comes to the other (v. 13).
- They glorify each other (vv. 1, 4-5, 24).
- One gives authority to the other (vv. 2, 7).
- One gave work, the other accomplished it (v. 4).
- One manifested the name of the other (vv. 6, 12, 26).
- One gave disciples to the other (vv. 6, 9).
- One gave words to the other, the other gave these words to men (vv. 8, 14).
- One asks the other (vv. 9, 15).
- One loves the other (vv. 4-5, 26).
- One knows the other (v. 5).

While we know from other passages that Jesus and God the Father are one in nature (e.g., John 5:18), this particular passage is not concerned with the doctrine of the Trinity. The above examples of oneness refer to a oneness and harmony of will, not a unity of nature, such as is in the Trinity. Therefore, the oneness that the disciples are to emulate is a oneness of purpose and will, not an identity in essence. Contrary to what pantheistic interpreters would have us believe, this passage is not teaching that disciples are one in nature with God. Note the distinctions made between Christ and the disciples in the context of this passage:

- One has authority over the other (v. 2).
- One gives eternal life to the other (v. 2).
- One should believe in the other (vv. 3, 7-8, 21, 25).
- One was given to the other (v. 6).
- One gave words of God to the other (vv. 8, 26).
- One asks on the other's behalf (vv. 9, 15, 20).
- One is glorified in the other (vv. 10, 22).
- One is no longer in the world while the other remains (v. 11).
- One guarded the other (v. 12).
- One has joy because of the other (v. 13).
- One is sanctified because of the other (v. 17).
- One sends the other (v. 18).
- One desires the other to be with Him (v. 24).

These distinctions make it apparent that Jesus was not referring to a oneness in nature or being, but a oneness in purpose and will. This fits the context of the disciples being commissioned at the time of this prayer (v. 18).

> They should seek God, if perhaps they might grope for Him and find Him, though He is not far from each one of us; for in Him we live and move and exist, as even some of your own poets have said, "For we also are His offspring." Being then the offspring of God, we ought not to think that the Divine Nature is like gold or silver or stone, an image formed by the art and thought of man. (Acts 17:27-29)

Even though this passage speaks of human beings living in God, it does not say we are God. The radical distinction between the world and God is maintained in the declaration of One creating the other (vv. 24-25) as well as establishing His decrees over mankind (v. 26). One is sought and the other seeks (v. 27); One calls for repentance, the other needs to repent (v. 30); One judges the other (v. 31); One has provided a way of righteousness for the other (v. 31). The point of contrast here is that which exists between God who created all things and things that were created. In other words, God is not a being that exists because of our imaginings and constructions, but He is a being who sustains our very existence.

There is one body and one Spirit, just as also you were called in one hope of your calling; one Lord, one faith, one baptism, one God and Father of all who is over all and through all and in all. (Eph. 4:4-6)

In response, two things should be pointed out. First, the theme of the Letter to the Ephesians is reconciliation and harmony between believers. Hence, the emphasis on oneness in these verses should be understood as referring to the relational oneness of harmony in purpose and will rather than a oneness of believers in God's being. Second, if this verse is to be taken pantheistically, then who is God the Father of? Fatherhood at least assumes children. But a pantheistic interpretation would imply that we are identical to God the Father and therefore, we are the Father of ourselves. This is clearly unacceptable logic.

The distinctiveness of God from the world must be maintained. As C. S. Lewis said,

> *Pantheism is a creed not so much false as hopelessly behind the times. Once, before creation, it would have been true to say that everything was God. But God created: He caused things to be other than Himself that, being distinct, they might learn to love Him, and achieve union instead of mere sameness.*[28]

Tragic Implications. Tom, one of Shirley MacLaine's spirit guides, told her that

> *If everyone was taught one basic spiritual law, your world would be a happier, healthier place. And that law is this: Everyone is God. Everyone. . . . When everyone is aligned with the knowledge that each is a part of God, the consciousness of civilization will reflect peace—peace within. Recognize that within each individual is the divine cosmic truth that you term God.*[29]

Supposedly, by recognizing the God within ourselves, we "will recognize the larger God-source, the magnificent energy which unites us all."[30] The New Ager thus reasons that this consciousness of being one in nature will lead to harmonious living. Mark Satin argues,

> *If we can't achieve a sense of oneness with nature, or the human race, or the cosmos, then chances are good that we'll try to "leave*

a mark on history" by following the path of least resistance to growth, or by advocating violent revolution, or by having lots and lots of children.[31]

Peace is brought about when one loves his neighbor as himself. How then does pantheism bring this about? Well, if pantheism is true, then "one's neighbor is one's self."[32] New Agers insist that peace and harmony will follow from a pantheistic conceptualization of our world.

There is a link between sorcery and pantheism. Of course, if one is God, then one can create, control, and manipulate reality. With all this power available to the pantheist, MacLaine reasons, "Maybe the tragedy of the human race was that we had forgotten we were each Divine."[33]

On the contrary, the real tragedy of the human race is that we delude ourselves into thinking that we are divine. Herbert Schlossberg, author of the penetrating work *Idols for Destruction,* writes that "if pantheism becomes as influential in the West as some observers expect," then we are about to witness its tragic effects. The influence of mysticism on German Protestantism "had the effect of destroying community and fellowship; communing with the 'vasty deep' within oneself makes ethics and concrete forms of social life superfluous."[34]

If unlimited potential emanates from within the depths of my being, then what need do I have for social reform? If all is one and the categories of good and evil are illusory, then what need have I for ethical decisions? If all is God and God is all, then what difference is there between a maggot and man, a worm and a woman?

The New Age movement wants Eastern ideology without Eastern sociology. It wants the Eastern deity without the same effect on Western society that pantheism has produced for centuries in impoverished India. Walk the streets of India, where social reform comes only from Western influences, and even then, ever so painfully slow. Pantheism "finds its rewards . . . in quietism, in surrender and union with the all-pervasive divinity that permeates nature." Accordingly, "the worshipers of such a divinity have populated Asia for centuries 'and have never dethroned the tyrant.' Introspection, self-isolation, and indifference derive naturally from such a theological position."[35]

G. K. Chesterton said, "Nature is not our mother, but our sister, and we do not need to bow down before her."[36] Creator and creation are not one. God and man are not the same. Man's problem is not that he does not realize he's divine. Man's problem is that he is tempted by the words of the serpent, "You will be like God" (Gen. 3:5).

"Scripture constantly makes it clear," wrote theologian G. C. Berkouwer, "that sin is not something which corrupts relatively or partially, but a corruption which fully affects the radix, the root, of man's existence, and therefore man himself."[37] Sinful man's obstacle to fulfillment is not divine amnesia, but alienation from the divine. The lost heart is alienated from "the life of God" (Eph. 4:18) until we are reconciled with God through the sacrificial death of Christ (Col. 1:21; Eph. 2:12-13).

In fact, the gospel presupposes the sinfulness of man. If there's nothing to be saved from, then there's no need for salvation. Any watering down of man's sinfulness, as New Agers attempt to do, dilutes the saving work of Christ.[38]

Small wonder that Francis Schaeffer said that the foundation of Christianity is the radical distinction between the Creator and the creature. If God and man are not distinct, then there can be no alienation, no separation between a holy God and sinful human beings. "So Christianity does not begin with 'accept Christ as Savior.' Christianity begins with 'In the beginning God created the heavens [the total cosmos] and the earth.' " This all adds up to the following: Accept pantheism and "you cannot maintain a true Christian position nor give Christianity's answers."[39]

Notes

1. For a detailed argument against pantheism, see Norman L. Geisler and William Watkins, *Perspectives: Understanding and Evaluating Today's Worldviews* (San Bernardino, Calif.: Here's Life, 1984), chap. 4.
2. Some New Agers are also pan-en-theists. Briefly, the difference is this: Pantheism means believing God is all, whereas pan-en-theism means believing God is *in* all. For a pantheist, God is identical to the real universe, but for the pan-en-theist God is simply in the universe the way a soul is in a body. But there is more to God than the actual changing universe. God also has a potential "pole" that goes beyond the universe. Despite the differences, both views unite in denying an infinite personal God beyond the universe who brought the universe into existence (as in theism). Both pantheism and panentheism hold a continuity between God and the universe, and both reject creation of the universe out of nothing.
3. Marilyn Ferguson, *The Aquarian Conspiracy* (Los Angeles: J. P. Tarcher, 1980), 100-101.
4. Mark Satin, *New Age Politics* (New York: Dell, 1979), 97.
5. David Spangler, *Revelation: The Birth of a New Age* (Findhorn, Scotland: Findhorn, 1978), 110, 121.

6. *The Upanishads: Breath of the Eternal,* trans. Swami Prabhavananda and Frederick Manchester (New York: Mentor, 1957), 45. Hindu scholar Sarvepali Radhakrishnan said, "We have (1) the Absolute, (2) God as Creative power, (3) God immanent in this world. These are not to be regarded as separate entities. They are arranged in this order because there is a logical priority." In *The Principal Upanishads* (London: Allen & Unwin, 1958), i.

7. E. A. Burtt, ed., *The Teachings of the Compassionate Buddha* (New York: New American Library, 1982), 195-196, 200.

8. C. S. Lewis, *Miracles: A Preliminary Study* (New York: Macmillan, 1947, 1960), 82-83.

9. Shirley MacLaine, *Out on a Limb* (New York: Bantam, 1983), 264.

10. Shirley MacLaine, *Dancing in the Light* (New York: Bantam, 1985), 103-104.

11. Ibid., 111.

12. Ibid., 354.

13. Ibid., 358.

14. Benjamin Creme, *Messages from Maitreya the Christ,* vol. 1, no. 98 (Los Angeles: Tara, 1980), 204.

15. MacLaine, *Out on a Limb,* 347.

16. MacLaine, *Dancing in the Light,* 133.

17. Ibid., 354-355.

18. Ibid., 362.

19. Ibid., 259.

20. Ibid., 265.

21. Ibid., 256.

22. Ibid., 357.

23. Geisler and Watkins, *Perspectives,* 92-93.

24. Francis Schaeffer, *The Complete Works of Francis A. Schaeffer: A Christian Worldview,* 5 vols. (Westchester, Ill.: Crossway, 1982), 1:110.

25. Rabindranath R. Maharaj with Dave Hunt, *Death of a Guru* (Nashville: Holman, 1977), 104.

26. Norman L. Geisler, *Christian Apologetics* (Grand Rapids: Baker, 1976), 189.

27. Gleason L. Archer, *Encyclopedia of Bible Difficulties* (Grand Rapids, Mich.: Zondervan, 1982), 374. "One additional observation is in order concerning this occasional employment of Elohim in the Old Testament to refer to believers under the covenant. This seems to operate by the analogy of national designations like *bene Yisra'el* ('the sons of Israel'), *bene Ammon* ('the sons of Ammon'), *bene Yehudah* ('the sons of Judah'), *bene Babel* ('the sons of Babylon'), etc. Any or all of these tribes or nations could also be referred to without the *bene* ('sons of'), as *Yisra'el, Ammon,* or *Yehudah.* By analogy, then, the combination *bene elohim* could be shortened to simple *elohim* alone—i.e., a member of the sons (or people) of God."

28. C. S. Lewis, *The Problem of Pain* (New York: Macmillan, 1962), 150-151.

29. MacLaine, *Dancing in the Light,* 412.

30. Ibid., 298.

31. Mark Satin, *New Age Politics* (New York: Dell, 1979), 97.

32. MacLaine, *Dancing in the Light,* 266.

33. MacLaine, *Out on a Limb,* 347.

34. Herbert Schlossberg, *Idols for Destruction* (Nashville: Thomas Nelson, 1983), 163.
35. Ibid.
36. Ibid., 176.
37. G. C. Berkouwer, *Man: The Image of God* (Grand Rapids: Eerdmans, 1962), 140-141.
38. Berkouwer, 144.
39. Schaeffer, *Complete Works,* 1:181, 114.

THREE
MANIPULATION OR MAGIC?
Dabbling with the Occult

In an interview on "The Phil Donahue Show," Shirley MacLaine said, "I'm what you call a good witch." When she began her exploration into Eastern thought, she "tried to keep an open mind" because she found herself confronted with what she earlier would have considered "science fiction" or "the occult."[1]

The word *occult* literally means "hidden." According to MacLaine, the occult is simply the methods by which one brings "hidden truth" to the conscious mind. She believes that this surfacing of hidden truth unleashes infinite potential. She says, "When you get in touch with your spiritual potential everything opens up—if that's witchcraft, then I'm for it."[2] She claims, "We are all psychics, we just don't know it."[3]

Man's attraction and fascination with the occult comes from an intense "human hunger for power."[4] *The Encyclopedia of Magic and Superstition* says that

> Magic has kept its long hold on the human mind because of the promise of power, which it holds out, however delusively, to each one of us, the prospect of spiritual mastery in the shape of the all-encompassing divine power which religion reserves of Almighty God alone.[5]

MacLaine claims that in a previous life she mastered the knowledge of weather control.[6] Down through history, occultists have claimed to be able to influence the weather:

> *At all times magicians, witches, and ecstatics of various kinds have been credited with influencing the weather; not only the shaman tying knots in his rope, but also the witches in their magical rituals, flying through the air on their broomsticks. They swept along among the clouds, they brought mists, they threw the hail, they were able to charm the winds on the ocean so that they could float to sea in a sieve.*[7]

In another past life MacLaine had the power to communicate with elephants and other animals of the jungle—kind of a Shirley Sheena.[8] "I felt the exquisite power of communication on both a collective and individual basis. It was an astonishing sensation of playfully benevolent power," she writes.[9]

"Omnipotence unqualified, supreme power over all things, is the ultimate goal of magic."[10] And even though MacLaine presumes to be "a good witch," witchcraft expert Frank Smyth writes, "The magician, black, white, or neutral, uses his art in a search for power. . . . He is constantly attempting to 'eat of the forbidden fruit' and 'be as God.' "[11]

The Scriptures do not deny the reality of supernormal evil. Paul writes in 2 Thessalonians 2:9 about "the one whose coming is in accord with the activity of Satan, with all power and signs and false wonders" (see Rev. 13:13; 16:14). Jesus assumed the reality of supernormal evil when He said, "Many will say to Me on that day, 'Lord, Lord, did we not prophesy in Your name, and in Your name cast out demons, and in Your name perform many miracles?' And then I will declare to them, 'I never knew you; depart from Me, you who practice lawlessness' " (Matt. 7:22-23).

However, the Bible does warn us against the one who "uses divination, one who practices witchcraft, or one who interprets omens, or a sorcerer, or one who casts a spell, or a medium, or a spiritist, or one who calls up the dead." Moses tells us in Deuteronomy 18:10-12 that "whoever does these things is detestable to the Lord" (2 Kings 21:6; Gal. 5:20).

The reality of demonic power should remind us that "our struggle is not against flesh and blood, but against the rulers, against the powers, gainst the world forces of this darkness, against the spiritual forces of wickedness in the heavenly places" (Eph. 6:12).

DIVINATION

Divination is the practice of foretelling future events or discovering hidden knowledge by occult means. This is usually accomplished by astrology, palmistry, card laying, visions, ouija boards, crystal balls, and an assortment of magic objects.

Hollywood guru Shirley MacLaine often tapped into the energy she inherited on her birthday due to a certain configuration of the sun and planets. [12] "The Babylonians and Assyrians connected their gods with the planets, and in the later classical world the universe as a whole was generally believed to be alive and divine, and the sun, moon, and planets were regarded as deities." Man was viewed as a microcosm of this divine universe. Therefore, since the gods were believed to "have their counterparts in human beings . . . their movements in the sky [were believed to] influence human character and behavior." [13] Thus was born the ancient practice of astrology.

Scripture warns us against the worship of celestial bodies in Deuteronomy 4:19. In Isaiah 47:13-15, God says that "the astrologers, those who prophesy by the stars, those who predict by the new moons," cannot save us because they cannot even save themselves (see Jer. 10:2-5).

Shirley MacLaine also admits to using magic stones[14] and power crystals. [15] Many New Agers believe that if you concentrate hard enough you can "program" crystals as you would a computer. Accordingly, both physical and spiritual problems can be healed through these "power rocks." Many celebrities—jazz trumpeter and record producer Herb Alpert, for example—have made fantastic claims for crystals' power to heal, to give inner tranquility, and even to affect erratic car engines. Crystals are a popular item in New Age bookstores and in many department and jewelry stores. They have become a key symbol for the New Age movement. But using such objects is clearly prohibited in Deuteronomy 18:10-12 (see 2 Kings 21:6). Such practices are contrary to God's ways. God tells us in Hosea 4:12 that to consult wooden idols and diviners' wands is to depart from God.

Divination has its source in the demonic. In Acts 16 we have the account of the slave girl who had a "spirit of divination." However, her ability for fortune-telling ceased when Paul cast a demon out of her in the name of Jesus (v. 18).

God is the only one who can reveal never-fail prophesy. God alone is sovereign over time and space. According to Isaiah 44:24-25, God often causes "the omens of boasters to fail, making fools out of diviners." In Zechariah 10:2 we find that diviners often produce "lying visions, and tell false dreams."

Christians must not come under the grip of Satan, whether it be through crystals or a rabbit's foot. All comfort and security should not come from divination, but from the Divine One (God).

VISUALIZATION

From business motivation seminars to Christian imaging, the ancient art of visualization is rising in popularity. Visualization techniques are based on the assumption that reality is only what we perceive it to be. MacLaine expresses this belief:

> *Perhaps reality was only what one believed it to be anyway. That would make all perceived realities real.*[16]

> *I was, in effect, living inside of my own reality, and so was everyone else.*[17]

> *Again there was no such thing as reality, only perception.*[18]

> *I could only say that we are not victims of the world we see. We are victims of the way we see the world.*[19]

Now if reality is only what we perceive it to be, then it follows that if we change our perception, we will change reality. Externally, MacLaine believes that she caused trees to sway.[20] One of her spirit guides told her that "the mind of man can influence nature, like earthquakes and flooding."[21]

Internally, we are what we think. Her channeler of spirit guides told her, "You are the result of your own thought. We all are. What we think is what we are. If you believe you are good and God is total love and God is in you, then your personal behavior patterns will express that belief."[22]

But as David Hunt and T. A. McMahon have pointed out in their book *The Seduction of Christianity*, occult "sorcery" is defined as "any attempt to manipulate reality . . . by various mind-over-matter techniques."[23] The sorcerer believes that he "is the cosmos in miniature" and therefore, "he can control cosmic forces by manipulating his own inner ideas and drives."[24]

Now, by "visualization" we are not referring to the many legitimate uses of the imagination, such as imagining the design of a house or painting, rehearsing a routine in your mind, or picturing an event in a book.[25] All of these uses of the imagination retain a distinction between the model in one's mind and the reality independent of the mind. On the other hand, occult visualization attempts to *manipulate* reality through the mind.

Visualization thus "elevates the human mind to godhood."[26] MacLaine boldly suggests, "*You* are the architect of your personal experience."[27] Notice that *she* is the architect, not God. Visualization places man on the throne of sovereignty because it attempts to rearrange what God has ordained and sovereignly decreed.

In contrast, as He did in Job 39:26-27 and 40:8-9, God would ask those who question His sovereignty,

> *Is it by your understanding that the hawk soars, stretching his wings toward the south? Is it at your command that the eagle mounts up, and makes his nest on high? . . . Will you really annul My judgment? Will you condemn Me that you may be justified? Or do you have an arm like God, and can you thunder with a voice like His?*

Visualization is not only an occult practice; it not only elevates man into godhood and displaces God's sovereignty, but it can lead to a confusion between the real and the unreal. Like some people who play fantasy role-playing games such as Dungeons and Dragons,[28] MacLaine is "confused about whether there is such a thing as actual 'reality.' "[29] And she often "wondered if [her] visualization was real or fantasy."[30]

Oddly enough, if reality is merely our perception, then there is no distinction between reality and perception anyway! And if there is no distinction between reality and perception, then how would MacLaine know if she was confused or not? In other words, MacLaine's very confusion about what is reality and what is perception demonstrates that there is a real difference between reality and perception. What you "see" is not always what you get.

SPIRIT GUIDES

In recent times we have gone from the fame of *Ghostbusters* to Shirley MacLaine — the "Ghosthustler." A large part of Shirley MacLaine's going *Out on a Limb* so that she could be *Dancing in the Light* involved contacting spirit guides.[31] Spirit guides are channeled through "mediums" — sort of "human telephones" (called "transchannelers") to the spirit realm.

Many of MacLaine's spirit guides appeared through Kevin Ryerson.[32] MacLaine explained the way in which spirit guides used "the electromagnetic frequencies of Kevin's body as a channel through which they could communicate" with her when Kevin went into a trance.[33]

These spirits are usually former human beings. MacLaine speaks with fondness about Ramtha, who turned out to be her brother in a past life.[34] And when her father was gravely ill, she comfortingly told him, "If you want to go — go ahead. Then you can help both of us [referring to her brother Warren Beatty and herself] from the other side. Maybe you'll be one of those spiritual guides I talk to."[35]

But MacLaine also refers to spirit guides who have never lived as humans. "Sometimes spiritual beings come through who have never incarnated at all."[36]

One of the ways in which these beings are said to benefit the "ghosthustler" is by providing information. For example, spirit guide Tom McPherson told MacLaine about her past lives[37] as well as consulted another spirit guide who specialized in nutrition.[38] Spirit guides even gave a diagnosis for cancer treatment.[39] McPherson told MacLaine that she was going to receive "a very fine script about a mother-and-daughter relationship and the opening shot of the film will be that of a child's clown" and even foresaw her winning of the Oscar for her role in that film.[40] (The film, as it turned out, was the acclaimed *Terms of Endearment,* and MacLaine did win the Best Actress Oscar.) The authenticity of her spirit guides were confirmed when they revealed "intimate details" about her life "which no other human being on earth knew."[41]

Another benefit of contacting spirits is their channeling of power. When MacLaine was exhausted and on the verge of collapse before a dance show, she pleaded with her spirit guides, "Come in and help me. . . . You have my permission to infuse your energies with mine." Slowly, she felt her arms "energize. A permeating glow ran through them." She visualized the light aura of Ramtha and McPherson mingling with hers.[42] She literally gave a power-packed performance.

Christians do not debate the possibility of contacting spirits, nor their power. Christians instead argue that such contacts are neither biblical nor wise. God warns us against contacting spirits in Leviticus 19:31, and Deuteronomy 18:10-12, as well as 2 Kings 21:6. In fact, in the Old

Testament age, God even commanded the death penalty for such practices in Leviticus 20:6, 27. First Chronicles 10:13-14 tells us that because Saul contacted dead Samuel through the witch of Endor (1 Sam. 28:3, 7-15) he was killed.

Our troubles should not be taken to spirits who are probably demons in disguise. Isaiah stated in 8:19, "And when they say to you, 'Consult the mediums and the spiritists who whisper and mutter,' should not a people consult their God? Should they consult the dead on behalf of the living?"

The key to wise living is found in the spiritual realm; not in dead spirits, but in the living God; and discovered not through so-called human telephones, but through divine letters recorded in the Bible.

CURE FOR DEMONIC POSSESSION/OPPRESSION

We are told in Scripture that in the last days, there will be an abundance of demonic activity. Paul tells us in 1 Timothy 4:1 "that in later times some will fall away from the faith, paying attention to deceitful spirits and doctrines of demons" (see 2 Pet. 2:1; Jude 4).

Because "the god of this world has blinded the minds of the unbelieving, that they might not see the light of the gospel of the glory of Christ" (2 Cor. 4:4; 2 Tim. 2:26), John tells us in 1 John 4:1 not to "believe every spirit, but test the spirits to see whether they are from God; because many false prophets have gone out into the world."

If an unbeliever is possessed by a demon, then he or she must realize that the cure does not come from ghosthustlers but is based on the sacrificial death of Jesus Christ (Col. 2:14-15).

The first step for the unbeliever plagued by demonic possession is to trust in Jesus for his salvation (John 1:12; Col. 1:13). Deliverance from a demon is a biblical function and should be done only in the name of Jesus as Paul did in Acts 16:16-18 (see Acts 5:16; Matt. 10:1; Jude 9).

But if we place our trust in Jesus Christ as Savior, we are then protected from demonic ownership since we are eternally and securely possessed by Christ (1 Cor. 6:19-20). However, Christians are still vulnerable to demonic oppression just as we are still vulnerable to our own lusts and the enticements of the world (1 John 2:16; James 1:14-15). Scripture gives us several steps to take when we are trying to free ourselves from occult bondage.

1. Confess our sins (1 John 1:9).
2. Renounce the works of the devil (2 Cor. 4:2).

3. Destroy occult objects. Even though it meant the loss of a large sum of money, many of the Ephesians "who practiced magic brought their books together and began burning them in the sight of all" (Acts 19:17-20; 2 Chron. 14:2-5; 23:17).

4. Break fellowship with occultists. Paul advises us in 2 Corinthians 6:14-16, "Do not be bound together with unbelievers; for what partnership have righteousness and lawlessness, or what fellowship has light with darkness? Or what harmony has Christ with Belial, or what has a believer in common with an unbeliever? Or what agreement has the temple of God with idols?" After being firmly grounded in the Word, we should continue to witness to occultists, but not seek their fellowship. We should influence them, not the other way around.

5. While we should resist the devil (James 4:7), Scripture tells us to flee temptation (1 Cor. 6:18; 10:14; 1 Tim. 6:11; 2 Tim. 2:22). If we used to be in the occult, then we should not tempt ourselves by watching occult movies, playing occult games, or reading occult books.

6. Meditate on and apply the Word of God (Eph. 6:17; Matt. 4:4, 7, 10). We should live in accordance with biblical truth, not in the bondage of the Father of lies (John 8:44).

7. Pray about it with other believers (Eph. 6:18; Matt. 18:19).

Our struggle against the powers of darkness is real and can be overbearing. But we also have comfort in knowing that we will "overcome them; because greater is He who is in [us] than he who is in the world" (1 John 4:4).

Notes

1. Shirley MacLaine, *Out on a Limb* (New York: Bantam, 1983), 5.
2. "The Phil Donahue Show," September 1985.
3. Shirley MacLaine, *Dancing in the Light,* (New York: Bantam, 1985), 123.
4. *Encyclopedia of Magic and Superstition* (London: Octopus, 1974), 13.
5. Ibid., 14.
6. MacLaine, *Dancing in the Light,* 331.
7. *Encyclopedia of Magic and Superstition,* 245.
8. MacLaine, *Dancing in the Light,* 370.
9. Ibid., 371.
10. *Encyclopedia of Magic and Superstition,* 11.
11. *Witchcraft, Magic, and the Supernatural* (London: Octopus, 1974), 133, 135.
12. MacLaine, *Dancing in the Light,* 29.
13. *Encyclopedia of Magic and Superstition,* 12.
14. MacLaine, *Out on a Limb,* 311.

15. MacLaine, *Dancing in the Light,* 8, 333.
16. MacLaine, *Out on a Limb,* 347.
17. MacLaine, *Dancing in the Light,* 121.
18. Ibid., 124.
19. Ibid., 121.
20. Ibid., 353.
21. Ibid., 264-265.
22. Ibid., 259.
23. Dave Hunt and T. A. McMahon, *The Seduction of Christianity* (Eugene, Oreg.: Harvest House, 1985), 12.
24. *Encyclopedia of Magic and Superstition,* 12.
25. Hunt and McMahon, *Seduction,* 123, 173.
26. Ibid., 109.
27. MacLaine, *Dancing in the Light,* 117.
28. It is often difficult for FRP (Fantasy Role Playing) players to distinguish between reality and fantasy. Often when an alter ego is killed, "the game player sometimes suffers psychic shock and may go into depression" (John Eric Holmes, "Confessions of a Dungeon Master," *Psychology Today* 14 (November 1980):93). Dungeon Master John Holmes admits that "The make-believe world assumes an eerie sense of reality" (Ibid., 93). "The stuff that makes me [Lee Gold, publisher of *Alarums and Excursions,* a communications magazine for FRP fans] nervous . . . is overidentification with characters. I've seen people have fits, yell for fifteen minutes, hurl dice at a grand piano when their character dies" (Moira Johnson, "It's Only a Game—Or Is It?" *New West,* 25 August 1980, 39).
29. MacLaine, *Out on a Limb,* 287.
30. Ibid., 289.
31. MacLaine, *Dancing in the Light,* 255.
32. MacLaine, *Out on a Limb,* 184.
33. MacLaine, *Dancing in the Light,* 80.
34. Ibid., 125-126.
35. Ibid., 61-62.
36. Ibid., 81.
37. Ibid., 269.
38. Ibid., 271.
39. Ibid., 415.
40. Ibid., 134, 126.
41. Ibid., 80, 127.
42. Ibid., 129.

FOUR
MANY HAPPY RETURNS?
The Reincarnation Fixation[1]

After "many happy returns"[2] as a prostitute, as her own daughter's daughter, a beheaded male court jester, a harem dancer, a monk, a Russian ballet dancer, a Brazilian voodoo practitioner, a Chinese tai chi artist, an Incan youth in Peru, and a host of other past lives, actress Shirley MacLaine has become the most popular proponent of reincarnation in recent times.[3] Following her best-selling book *Out on a Limb,* which covered her introduction to reincarnation, MacLaine enjoyed the success of her more occultic sequel, *Dancing in the Light.* Her 1987 television mini-series "Out on a Limb," based on her alleged reincarnation experiences, assured the mass introduction of Eastern thought into American culture.

Many other celebrities have revealed their belief in reincarnation, such as Sylvester "Rambo" Stallone,[4] country singer Loretta Lynn,[5] General George S. Patton,[6] automobile industrialist Henry Ford,[7] and American author Mark Twain.[8]

Late actor Peter Sellers of *Pink Panther* fame confided in MacLaine his belief in reincarnation. Sellers claimed that the reason he could perform his impersonations so well was that he had actually been those characters in past lives.[9] A year and a half later, when MacLaine was told that Peter Sellers had died, she said, "Yes, you probably think he's dead, but he's really only left his latest body."[10]

According to a 1982 Gallup poll, almost one in every four Americans believe in reincarnation,[11] even though nine out of every ten Americans claim Christianity as their religious preference.[12] This proportion increases to 30 percent among college age persons. Furthermore, about 17 percent of those who claim to attend church regularly also affirm their belief in reincarnation. The figures are even more surprising when one is confronted with statistics revealing that 21 percent of professing Catholics believe in reincarnation[13] in spite of the fact that the doctrine of reincarnation is officially condemned by Rome.

THE MEANING OF REINCARNATION

The word *reincarnation* comes from a combination of Latin words (*re* and *carne*) which literally means "to come again in the flesh."[14] World religions authority Geoffrey Parrinder defines reincarnation as "the belief that the soul or some power passes after death into another body."[15] There are many types of reincarnation views, but the New Age view is generally one that believes man is in an evolutionary progress toward perfection, which can only be achieved through reincarnations.

THE SO-CALLED PSYCHOLOGICAL EVIDENCE FOR REINCARNATION

A flight attendant dreaded having anything touch her neck. Discovering her past life as a victim of the guillotine cured her phobia. When grandpa reminisces about "the good ole days," we assume that he knows facts from those times because he was actually there. In the same way, many reincarnationists argue that the knowledge of facts from the past demonstrates that they once lived in that time period.

In most cases, giving facts about a time before birth has been explained without recourse to reincarnation. Through hypnosis, a woman supposedly regressed to old Ireland in the seventeenth or eighteenth century. She reportedly spoke Gaelic, described the coastline where she lived, discussed many of the customs and clothing, and even had a deep Irish accent. This became known as the Bridey Murphy case.

However, research turned up evidence that this woman was reared by Gaelic-speaking grandmother. Apparently her early nurturing in the Gaelic language and the history of old Ireland was forgotten as she grew older, but they were never totally erased from her memory.[16] This girl had mistakenly interpreted latent memories for a previous existence.

Reincarnationists sometimes use déjà vu, the feeling that a certain event took place before, as proof of a previous life. But déjà vu has been explained by what scientists call "cryptoamnesia." Cryptoamnesia is that process whereby a person forgets that she got her information from a past source and comes to believe that this information is a memory from a previous experience. At times, a certain conversation is so much like one that took place in the past that it seems that we had that identical conversation before.[17] Researchers have even found a possible physiological basis for déjà vu. When the data from the environment enters the eye, sometimes the transmission of this information to the brain is delayed for a micro-second; leading the person to believe that she had seen it before.[18]

Cultural conditioning also plays a large part in the so-called reincarnation findings. It's interesting that out of some three hundred alleged cases of past-life recall, over one hundred are from India.[19] Dr. Ian Stevenson, perhaps the most respected researcher of "cases suggestive of reincarnation," admits that the "principal sites of abundant reported cases" of reincarnation are in those cultures where there is a concentrated belief in reincarnation.[20]

However, in all fairness to Stevenson and others, there are cases which seem impossible to explain by purely naturalistic means. In the best cases, factual familiarity has often been verified, ruling out the chances for someone learning these facts from her parents, studies, or any other contrived fashion.

Such supernormal activities should be no surprise to the student of Scripture. The Bible affirms the reality of demonic oppression and possession (Matt. 8:30-34; Mark. 8:32-34; Luke 4:31-37; Acts 16:16-18; 19:11-16). The activity of demons could easily account for the incredible cases of past-life recall.

Even Edgar Cayce, the prophet of reincarnation, considered the possibility of demonic influence in his "revelations," which supported reincarnation. He said, "The Devil might be tempting me to do his work by operating through me when I was conceited enough to think God had given me special power. . . . If ever the Devil was going to play a trick on me, this would be it."[21] At best, past-life recall is a bizarre fad which preys upon gullible minds. At its worst, it is a hideous prank played by demonic forces.

REINCARNATION AND THE PROBLEM OF EVIL

One prominent reincarnationist has declared, "The strongest support of reincarnation is its happy solution of the problem of moral inequality and injustice and evil which otherwise overwhelms us as we survey the world."[22] This argument is interwoven with the doctrine of karma, which says that one's present condition was determined by his actions in a past life.

The reincarnationists' reasoning is that it would be unjust of God to make someone suffer when he did not deserve it. And many children and newborns suffer tragically before they could possibly have the moral capacity to commit a sin. Therefore, the reincarnationist argues, these unfortunate infants suffer because of sins they committed in past lives.

Why is one born in the lap of luxury while another is thrust into a miserable existence of poverty and pain? How do we reconcile the apparent injustices in the world? Are these "inequities" a thorn in the side of traditional Christianity?

The doctrine of karma and reincarnation basically says that just as one good turn deserves another, so also one bad turn (in one life) deserves another bad turn (in another life). But when will this cycle end? And how did it begin? With the problem of evil and karmic reincarnation, one would have to keep "backpedaling" to find the cause of evil. In a previous life, Shirley MacLaine claims that she was raped and had her throat slit. What did she do to deserve such a grisly fate? Well, in a life before that, she was a Roman guard who imprisoned an old woman and her daughter. This woman and daughter died of starvation and leprosy that was contracted from all of the filth in the dungeon. This woman was the young man who raped MacLaine in a subsequent life.[23]

Let's try to sort out these events in relation to the so-called reincarnationist explanation for the existence of evil and suffering in the world. MacLaine's reincarnational interpretation says that the reason why she was raped and murdered in one life was because she imprisoned and killed her rapist in a previous life. But then why did the rapist deserve to be imprisoned in the first place? Perhaps he was imprisoned because he abused his children in a past life. Then were his children abused because they ripped off Twinkies from the neighborhood grocery store?

We could go on backpedaling into infinity. But if you keep backpedaling forever, then you never arrive at the origin of evil. So how did evil begin? Under reincarnationist circumstances, there is no origin of evil. How did suffering begin in the first place if each life of suffering must be preceded by a past life of sin?

The reincarnationist answer to the problem of evil is repulsive to our moral sensitivities. Its so-called solution to the tragedy of innocent suffering is the assertion that anyone who suffers is not really innocent. Then why should we feel compassion for the rape victim if she truly deserved it because of a past evil? Why should a child born with birth defects receive care and comfort when he brought it upon himself? No wonder native Indian scholars themselves have blamed the doctrines of reincarnation and karma for the fatalism, lack of concern for the suffering of others, and general inaction in India.[24]

Reincarnationists do not honestly confront the issue of the origin of evil; they only eternally delay their answer. On the other hand, the Bible doesn't pass the buck to some former life.[25]

Much of our suffering is the result of decisions freely made in this life, either by oneself or by others. People make evil choices that affect themselves and others. Innocent people may get hurt in the process. "The early bird gets the worm," but the early worm also gets eaten. Tragic as our free choices may be for ourselves and others, free choice is an essential for a moral world. Robots have no moral duty, and they will receive no reward.

This may mean that trials and tragedies are divinely allowed so that we'll give up our independence from the One who created us and sustains our moment-to-moment existence. Sometimes the only way we will look up is if we are flat on our backs. And it may very well be that God's love for us is so strong that He'll permit the full measure of temporal pain if it will result in eternal pleasure.

Some suffering is also the by-product of good processes. For example, the lightning and rain that provide the right combination for a fertile land occasionally electrocute the person standing on it. The ocean offers a place not only for sailing and swimming, but also for drowning.

Further, suffering is designed to bring about virtues, such as patience and understanding in the face of tragedy. Courage is manifested in the midst of danger. There is a purpose for pain. As the adage goes, "no pain, no gain."

Even though our finite minds may be unable to think of a good reason for all the evil we encounter, this does not mean that an infinite being could not have some good reason. We should logically expect an unlimited mind to have reasons unknown to limited minds. And if limited minds can see some good reasons for the existence of evil, as we just did, then the probability of an infinite mind having good reasons for permitting evil increases.

The doctrine of reincarnation does not solve the problem of evil. Rather, the belief in reincarnation is part of the problem of evil. It offers false hopes, false alternatives to the truth, and can justify evil practices.

It is worth mentioning here that reincarnation offers a forceful illustration of the New Age movement's amazing inconsistency. Since most New Agers want to blur the distinction between good and evil, or even to claim that there is no such thing as good or evil, how can a person be punished or rewarded in a future life? If good and evil are not real (or if they are ultimately the same), it makes no sense to speak of karma and of reincarnation based on one's behavior.

THE INNER NEED FOR A SECOND CHANCE

Shirley MacLaine's mentor asked her, "What are you worried about? . . . You'll keep on playing parts until you finally get it right."[26] Many reincarnationists argue that in order for there to be justice and love in the cosmos, God must give us such a "second chance." Reincarnation thus eliminates the need for hell. We just keep coming back until we reach perfection. Surely a God of love would not punish us with endless hell just because we blow it in a single life?

But the love of God should not be understood apart from God's justice. The demands of divine love are intertwined with a deeply moral core. Jesus said, "If you love Me you will keep My commandments" (John 14:15). God is just, and so He cannot let sin go without punishment. This is tough love. A holy love, not namby-pamby love which arbitrarily discards justice.

If sin were to be just swept aside, then God would not truly be just and holy. Sin must be condemned by a holy God. Yet out of His mercy, God provided a way of escaping the wrath of that judgment. Since He is holy, the wrath must come. But because He is merciful, the wrath can be poured out on someone else—someone better able to endure the wrath of sin and someone so morally innocent and pure that He could justly pay for our sins. Out of God's holy love flows His gracious means by which our sins can be forgiven—namely, the payment of the sacrifice of His Son. And once a holy requirement (the death of Christ) is necessary for entrance into heaven, it would naturally follow that those who do not appropriate this requirement will not enter heaven. The Bible calls this non-heaven *hell*.

Hell is the alternative for those who choose to reject God. If they choose to decline God's gracious offer, then God will not unlovingly force them into His kingdom. G. K. Chesterton said, "Hell is the greatest compliment God has ever paid to the dignity of human freedom."[27]

There is no need for more than one opportunity to be saved. Reincarnationists use the illustration of the compassionate teacher who gives his student another chance to retake an exam. But we could just as well suggest the illustration of shooting oneself in the head. Some decisions in life are final. Not all trials in life afford limitless or even multiple opportunities. In fact, one could make a case that our experience shows that the amount of decisive opportunities decreases with the increasing weight of the decision. And the decision to accept or reject God's ultimate offer is surely the weightiest decision of all. For it is written in Hebrews 9:27, "It is appointed for men to die once and after this comes judgment."

And finally, reincarnation ultimately stands opposed to salvation by grace. Reincarnation assumes some notion of karma; that is, the notion that actions in a previous life have determined the conditions of my present reincarnation.

In other words, what one accomplishes in this life determines his condition in the next. This is essentially a salvation by works. The Christian believes that his salvation comes about after the choice to be saved by grace alone, not by the chores of self-effort (Eph. 2:8-10).

THE ALLEGED BIBLICAL SUPPORT
FOR REINCARNATION

Reincarnationists use the life of John the Baptist as an example of reincarnation in the Bible. Jesus affirmed in Matthew 11:14 and 17:10-13 (Mark 9:11-13; Luke 1:17) that Elijah had "already come" in the person of John the Baptist. This leads some reincarnationists to conclude that John the Baptist was therefore a reincarnation of Elijah.

But reincarnation theory says that the soul finds another body in which to incarnate after the body dies. And Elijah never died (2 Kings 2:11; cf. Heb. 11:5)! Luke 1:17 says that John was a forerunner of Christ "in the spirit and power of Elijah." The meaning of this verse is clearly seen from the story of Elijah in 2 Kings 2:9-18. Before Elijah's earthly departure, his disciple Elisha wishes to "inherit a double portion" of Elijah's "spirit." After the whirlwind had taken Elijah up, those standing by saw Elisha perform a miracle and said, "The spirit of Elijah rests on Elisha." This phrasing could not have meant that Elisha was the reincarnation of Elijah, since they both lived at the same time.

Coming "in the spirit and power of Elijah" is not a reference to a personal identity but to a functional similarity. So John was not the recipient of the soul of Elijah but of the power of Elijah. It should come as no surprise then, that when the Jewish leaders asked John if he was Elijah,

John plainly and emphatically denied it (John 1:21).

In John 3:3, Jesus answered Nicodemus, "Truly, truly, I say to you, unless one is born again, he cannot see the kingdom of God." Must you be born again . . . and again, and again? The Greek word for "again" has a double reference, meaning both "again" and "from above" (*anothen*). In verse 8 it is equated with being "born of the Spirit." This passage is not referring to a physical rebirth (reincarnation), but to a spiritual birth (conversion).

In John 9:1-3, Jesus saw a man blind from birth. His disciples asked Him, "Rabbi, who sinned, this man or his parents, that he should be born blind?" Jesus answered, "It was neither that this man sinned, nor his parents; but it was in order that the works of God might be displayed in him."

Some reincarnationists claim that the disciples were assuming that the man sinned in a previous life, thus resulting in his blindness. Jewish theologians at that time gave two reasons for birth defects: 1. prenatal sin (before birth, but not before conception) and 2. parental sin. They claimed that when a pregnant woman worshiped in a heathen temple, the fetus committed idolatry as well.[28] While it is unnecessary to subscribe to these ancient Jewish beliefs about prenatal sin, the point is that Jewish tradition contained the belief in prenatal sin, not reincarnation. And so it is reasonable to conclude that the disciples assumed a false belief of prenatal sin in accord with their religious tradition.

But even if the disciples assumed reincarnation, Christ plainly denied it in verse 3. He rejected the notion that the blindness had anything to do with the man's previous sin (v. 2).

Scripture does not support the belief in reincarnation. The reincarnated body is mortal, it will die again and again. Indeed, reincarnation occurs thousands and thousands of times. On the other hand, the resurrection body according to 1 Corinthians 15 is imperishable, immortal — it will never die. And what will never die cannot be reincarnated. Resurrection is a one-time event, never to be repeated. Reincarnation is a stutter-step process of rising only to fall again. But to be resurrected is to soar to the heights of glory, never to stumble, never to fall.

Notes

1. For a detailed treatment of the doctrine of reincarnation, see Norman L. Geisler and J. Yutaka Amano, *The Reincarnation Sensation* (Wheaton, Ill.: Tyndale House, 1986).

2. *"Many Happy Returns"* was the original title for MacLaine's sequel to *Out on*

a Limb, now titled *Dancing in the Light* (New York: Bantam, 1985), 28, 407.

3. MacLaine, *Dancing in the Light,* 383-384.

4. John Leo, "I Was Beheaded in the 1700s," *Time,* 10 September 1984, 68.

5. Loretta Lynn and George Vessey, "Loretta Lynn: Coal Miner's Daughter," *Time,* 10 September 1984, 68-69.

6. Maurice Rawlings, *Life Wish* (Nashville: Thomas Nelson, 1981), 5.

7. San Francisco *Examiner,* 28 August 1928, as cited in Joseph Head and S. L. Cranston, *Reincarnation in World Thought* (New York: Julian, 1967), 349.

8. "Simplified Spelling" in *Letters from the Earth,* ed. B. Deveto (New York: Harper and Row, 1962), 159.

9. MacLaine, *Out on a Limb,* 169.

10. Ibid., 173.

11. George Gallup, Jr., *Adventures in Immortality* (New York: McGraw-Hill, 1982), 192.

12. *Emerging Trends,* September 1982, 3.

13. Gallup, *Adventures in Immortality,* 202.

14. Peter A. Angeles, *Dictionary of Philosophy* (New York: Barnes and Noble, 1981), 243.

15. Geoffrey Parrinder, *Dictionary of Non-Christian Religions* (Philadelphia: Westminster, 1971), 286.

16. Harry Rosen, *A Scientific Report on the Search for Bridey Murphy* (New York: Julian, 1956) and Martin Gardner, *Fads and Fallacies* (New York: Dover, 1974).

17. Rawlings, *Life Wish,* 103.

18. Ibid.

19. C. T. K. Chari, "Some Critical Considerations Concerning Karma and Rebirth," *Indian Philosophical Annual* (1965):132-133; John H. Hick, *Death and Eternal Life* (New York: Harper and Row, 1976), 374-375.

20. Ian Stevenson, "The Explanatory Value of the Idea of Reincarnation," *Journal of Nervous and Mental Disease* 164 (1977):305-326.

21. Thomas Sugue, *The Story of Edgar Cayce: There Is a River,* rev. ed. (Virginia Beach: Association for Research and Enlightenment, 1973), 210.

22. E. D. Walker, *Reincarnation: A Study of Forgotten Truth* (New Hyde Park, N.Y.: University Books, 1965), 34.

23. MacLaine, *Dancing in the Light,* 396.

24. Kana Mitra, "Human Rights in Hinduism," *Journal of Ecumenical Studies,* Summer 1982, 84.

25. For a more detailed treatment of the problem of evil from a Christian perspective, see Norman L. Geisler, *Roots of Evil* (Grand Rapids: Zondervan, 1978).

26. MacLaine, *Out on a Limb,* 297.

27. Quoted in Leighton Ford, *Christ the Liberator* (Downers Grove, Ill.: InterVarsity, 1971), cited in Kerby Anderson's *Life, Death and Beyond* (Grand Rapids: Zondervan, 1980), 167.

28. Herman L. Strack and Paul Billerbeck, *Kommentar zum Nuen Testament aus Talmud und Midrash* (Munich: Straek and Billerbeek, 1961), 2:527-529; Raymond E. Brown, *The Gospel According to John,* 2 vols. (Garden City, N.Y.: Doubleday, 1966), 1:371.

FIVE
ESTEEM OR DEIFICATION?
The Obsession with Self

Today, a hamburger is served "my way." According to other television commercials, I should color my hair "because I'm worth it" and drink ice tea "because I believe in me." We live in a society that markets self-centeredness. No wonder we are quick to embrace a psychology—and religion—of selfism.

THE DANGERS OF SELF-DEIFICATION
It seems that "Western psychologists and psychiatrists are the gurus of the 1980s," often "leading us into New Age mysticism."[1] From psychologists like Abraham Maslow, Erich Fromm, and Carl Rogers to business seminars like the Forum and Silva Mind Control—all advocate the release of the supposed unlimited potential within us in order to solve our problems.

Self-deification is the gospel of the New Age. Man, the New Agers tell us, has divine amnesia. Humans, they say, have forgotten somehow that the divine is found within.

Then why do we have so many problems? According to the self-help salesmen of selfism, our problems are caused by external forces like traditional religion and moral absolutes. Religion hinders our effectiveness, productivity, and fulfillment by stressing the negative aspect of our nature.

The doctrine of sin, for example, must be relegated to the status of ancient mythology. New Age psychology tells us that humans do not have sin natures. We are supposedly filled with "the possibility of being" — being anything we want to be. Thus we are told to elevate self and actualize our divine potential.

Popular psychology has moved away from its secular roots without abandoning its humanistic nature. Ready to accept and even cultivate religious ideas, New Age psychology simply enlarges its humanism to cosmic proportions. "The old-fashioned secular humanist . . . said, 'There is no Deity. Long live humanity.' [But] The new transpersonal or cosmic humanist says, 'There is no Deity but humanity.' God is pulled into the human breast."[2]

Unfortunately, this selfist psychology has crept into the church as well. Apologists against the New Age movement have claimed that "the seductive gospel of selfism is now preached by prominent pastors and proclaimed by well-known conference speakers."[3] We must admit that "Self is the predominant theme of a large percentage of Christian books and sermons."[4]

Many a pulpit has implicitly denied the biblical truth of our sin nature as well as our tendency to elevate self to godhood. "What used to be called pride is now called 'positive self-talk.' "[5]

Such New Age platitudes must be rejected. The gospel presupposes the need for salvation from sin. God said in Jeremiah 17:9 that "the heart is deceitful above all things, and desperately wicked." Paul wrote in Romans 3:23 that "all have sinned and fall short of the glory of God."[6] Paul also warned us against New Age psychology in 2 Timothy 3:2 where he cautions the church about "lovers of self."

Christian psychologist Paul Vitz says that "the relentless and single-minded search for and glorification of the self is at direct cross purposes with the Christian injunction to lose the self. . . . The Christian knows that the self is the problem, not the potential paradise."[7]

In fact, some recent psychological research challenges the claims of the psychology of selfism. Evidence accumulated by psychologist David G. Myers has demonstrated that the essential problem with man is not that he thinks too little of himself, but too much.[8] "Unless we close our eyes to a whole river of evidence, it . . . seems that the most common error in people's self-images is not unrealistically low self-esteem, but rather a self-serving bias; not an inferiority complex, but a superiority complex."[9]

In Philippians 2:1-4, Paul urges us to think of others before ourselves. Chuck Swindoll put it this way:

*Yourself, yourself, yourself. We're up to here with self! Do some-
thing either for yourself or with yourself or to yourself. How very
different from Jesus' model and message! No "philosophy" to turn
our eyes inward, He offers rather a fresh and much-needed invi-
tation to our "me-first" generation. There is a better way. Jesus says,
"Be a servant, give to others!"*[10]

BACKFIRING INTO PANTHEISM

As bad as the psychology of selfism is, many persons, in their zeal to
refute New Age psychology, ironically find themselves backing into a
kind of New Age view of God. In an overreaction to the psychology of
selfism, Hunt and McMahon seem to reject any notion of self-esteem.
"The Bible never urges self-acceptance, self-love, . . . self-confidence,
self-esteem . . . nor any of the other selfisms that are so popular
today." [11]

There is no room for a middle ground, according to Hunt and McMahon. They claim that "to whatever extent we focus upon a self-image,
no matter how sincerely, we are robbing ourselves and God of that relationship we must have with Him if we are rightly to reflect His
image." [12]

Foregoing a balanced view of self-esteem, Hunt and McMahon seem
to have come full circle. They denigrate the self to the point where we
could ask: "What place is there for the self?" Sure, the Bible teaches that
man is "dead in sin" (Eph. 2:1) and that the sinful self is "wretched" (Rom.
7:24), but we must be careful not to denigrate the self to the point where
there is no self and Christ is "exalted" to the point where He is all that
exists.

Could it be that the logic of this reasoning unwittingly leads in the direction of a New Age view itself? No, Dave Hunt is not a New Ager. And
yet, his overzealousness moves in the direction of the very view he himself abhors—namely that God is all, and all is God—the view of pantheism. Yes, men are wretched sinners and Christ should be proclaimed
throughout all the universe, but the biblical perspective brings balance
to these truths. The sinner is not so denigrated that his individuality and
worth become so swallowed up as to be, for all practical purposes, lost
in Christ. We must be careful. Arguments against those who advocate
having a positive self-image can be taken to such an extreme that they
boomerang into pantheism—the very thing Hunt wishes to defeat.

There is a serious flaw in Hunt's mirror analogy with the image of God in man. He claims that we should think about the image of God in man as we do a mirror. For a mirror "has one purpose only: to reflect a reality other than its own. It would be absurd for a mirror to try to develop a 'good self-image.' It is equally absurd and certainly unbiblical, for humans to attempt to do so."[13] If Hunt's words are taken seriously, they deny the reality of human nature that God created.

But what about the man or woman who embodies God's image? Where are they? Are they, like New Age pantheists, swallowed up into God? As R. C. Sproul wrote in his book *The Holiness of God,* "God's work of grace upon Isaiah's soul did not annihilate his personal identity. . . . Far from God seeking to destroy the 'self,' as many distortions of Christianity would claim, God redeems the self."[14]

We must avoid both the psychology of selfism and the psychology of self-contempt. Either direction steers us head-on toward a pantheistic view.

SELF-ESTEEM AND HUMILITY

Some writers confuse the biblical notion of humility with the lack of self-esteem. Dave Hunt's writings seem to imply that either we must be humble or have self-esteem.[15] He calls the identification of humility with self-esteem an "embarrassing contradiction." "One can only wonder, though, why high self-esteem is equated with humility—and whether low self-esteem, its opposite, is therefore the same as pride."[16]

Let's be clear: We are not equating humility with self-esteem. All we are saying is that humility is *compatible* with self-esteem. Second, to use "high" and "low" as qualifiers for self-esteem has built-in negative overtones and evades the issue. It is far more accurate to speak in terms of healthy and unhealthy self-esteem.

Why can't someone have both humility and self-esteem? Hunt's error seems to be that he wrongly identifies self-esteem with pride—which means he confuses self-esteem for pride.

Josh McDowell, in *His Image, My Image,* speaks of the difficulty Christians have in seeing the distinction between self-worth and pride.[17] But there is a real difference.

Self-worth is the conviction that we have value because of what God has done in us and for us. God created us in His image, and His Son died for our sins. On the other hand, pride is the presumption that our value lies in our own abilities and achievements.

Self-esteem should not be equated with pride. Proper self-esteem is part of being truly humble. To be humble before God is to recognize His superiority, His sovereignty, His ultimacy, but not to negate our identity or dignity. The passages in the Bible concerning humility never encourage us to perceive ourselves as totally worthless and without value.

We have to keep in mind the contrast in Scripture being made between sinful humans and a holy God. In comparison with God, our worth (which is derived from His goodness) is infinitesimal. Our value is "nothing" in comparison with the supreme value of God. But that is not the same thing as saying that we have no value at all. Just because the artistry of world-renowned pianist Peter Serkin is so magnificent that it overshadows others' feeble attempts does not mean that their ability is totally without value.

Humility, then, involves seeing the self honestly. We are not supreme. God is. Pride sees the self dishonestly—it balloons our actual limitations into so-called infinite potential. Humility is selfless and God-centered, while pride is selfish and self-centered. Loving oneself as a creature is good, but exalting oneself as the Creator is evil.

A healthy self-esteem means looking at the self honestly and recognizing that our worth is given to us by God. Therefore, someone with a healthy self-esteem can be biblically humble as well. "In Romans 12:3 Paul did not say that we should not think highly of ourselves. He said we should not think more highly of ourselves than what we really are." [18] He said, "I say to every man among you not to think more highly of himself than he ought to think; but to think so as to have sound judgment" (Rom. 12:3).

A BALANCED VIEW OF SELF-ESTEEM

While there are many passages in Scripture that confirm the presence of our sin nature, there are also many verses that affirm man's intrinsic value and how he ought to love himself.

At creation, man was deemed to be good (Gen. 1:31) because he was created in the image of God (Gen. 1:27). And Genesis 9:6 and James 3:9 make it clear that man did not lose the image of God even after the Fall. Scripture maintains that man is neither completely good nor entirely evil. Humans are not ultimately worthy as New Agers say, but we are not completely worthless either.

Our Worth before God. The logic of God loving us is that we must be lovable. [19] God's great concern for little creatures is nothing in comparison to how much value He places on us (Matt. 6:26; 10:31; Luke 12:7). Hunt questions this reasoning: "Does it really build self-esteem to be told that we are worth more than such insignificant birds?" He argues that "it is one thing to ascribe worth to self because of God's love and another thing entirely to realize that God loves us not because of who we are but because of who He is (God is love)." [20]

But this rationale poses a false either/or situation. Hunt would like us to think that either God loves us because of who we are or He loves us because of who He is. But both claims are true. God loves us because of who we are (creatures in God's image) and because of who He is. Hunt has devised an argument to polarize these truths when they do not logically exclude each other.

Obviously, Hunt's main point of contention is that God doesn't love us because of who we are. But then, if it doesn't matter who we are, then it wouldn't matter if we were sparrows. In other words, there would be no distinction between God's love for sparrows and humans. But this would be contrary to Scripture which affirms that God places more value on us than on the other creatures of the earth (Gen. 1:27-28; Ps. 8:3-8; Matt. 6:26; 10:31).

Of all creatures, from every kind of animal to each and every angelic being, man is the sole object of redemption (John 3:16). Right now the Lord Jesus Christ prepares a place for us in eternity (John 14:1-3). The psalmist was not boasting in himself when he sang, "I praise You because I am fearfully and wonderfully made; Your works are wonderful" (Ps. 139:14). As McDowell wrote, "A healthy self-image is 'seeing yourself as God sees you—no more and no less.' " [21]

Our Value according to the Cross. Not only are we worthy because we were created worthy, but our self-worth

> *is interwoven into the heart of God's redemptive process. The One who bought us with a price knows our true worth. The price He paid for you and me is Jesus (1 Cor. 6:20; 1 Pet. 1:18-19). If you ever did put out a price tag on yourself, it would have to read "Jesus." His death on the cross was the payment for our sins. You are "worth Jesus" to God because that is what He paid for you. That is His statement of your value. And God's view of you and your worth is the true one.* [22]

In James Dobson's best-selling book *Hide or Seek,* he said that "the most valuable contribution a parent can make to his child is to instill in him a genuine faith in God." What better way to see myself than to realize that the One who knows more than all the knowledge contained in the universe — knows me! Personally, intimately, totally. He who possesses the riches of the world values me to the point of sending His Son as a sacrifice on my behalf. "What a beautiful philosophy with which to 'clothe' your tender child. What a fantastic message of hope and encouragement for the broken teenager who has been crushed by life's circumstances."[23]

Self-love Assumed in Loving Our Neighbors. Proper self-esteem is based on God's acts of creation and redemption. It is also presupposed by His moral decree. We are commanded "Love your neighbor as yourself" six times in Scripture.[24] Thus, loving others assumes that we love ourselves. The Bible assumes "a normal, natural self-love, rather than telling us to hate ourselves."[25] Indeed, Paul encourages a wholesome self-love, saying, "No one ever hated his own body, but he feeds and cares for it, just as Christ does the church — for we are members of His body" (Eph. 5:30-31).

And even if the biblical injunctions are not commands for self-love, they assume that there is a sense in which self-love is right. Apparently, "self-love is the basis of loving others." The implication is that we cannot even love others unless we love ourselves. If we cannot respect the good God created in us, then how can we be expected to respect the good of God's creation elsewhere?

In any case, there seems to be an innate contradiction within circles where the gospel of self-hate is taught. If I am so contemptible a creature, then why should I be so sadistic as to force my wretched company upon other people? Why should I despise the one self, namely me, while at the same time holding in esteem all other selves — being no less horrid?[26]

A biblical view of self-esteem is based on the fact that God created me in His image and sent His Son to die for my sins, and is assumed in the great undertaking of loving my neighbor.

Self-Denial and Self-Affirmation. Hunt tells us that "one cannot deny self and at the same time love, esteem, and accept self."[27] However, the Bible seems to teach both self-denial (Mark 8:34) *and* self-affirmation (Matt. 6:26; Ps. 139:14). John Stott tells us to look to the cross of Christ for the answer to harmonizing these two great truths.[28] Jesus denied His self in one sense and yet retained it in another.

Our personal identity is a dynamic composite that "is partly the result of the Creation (the image of God), and partly the result of the Fall (the image defaced)." Therefore, we must deny that part of our self which follows the way of Adam—fallen man—and affirm that part within us which follows Christ the perfect man. Whatever is incompatible with Christ must be discarded ("Let him deny himself and follow me"). Whatever is compatible with Christ should be embraced ("he who loses his life will find it"). Hence, true self-denial (the denial of our evil, fallen self) is not the road to self-destruction, but the road to self-discovery.

Stott details those items in our lives which

> we must affirm: our rationality, our sense of moral obligation, our masculinity and femininity, our aesthetic appreciation and artistic creativity, our stewardship of the fruitful earth, our hunger for love and community, our sense of the transcendent mystery of God, and our in-built urge to fall down and worship him.[29]

Recognizing that we have been "tainted and twisted by sin," we need to affirm what Christ seeks to redeem and reclaim. On the other hand,

> we must deny or repudiate: our irrationality; our moral perversity; our loss of sexual distinctives; our fascination with the ugly; our lazy refusal to develop God's gifts; our pollution and spoilation of the environment; our selfishness, malice, individualism, and revenge, which are destructive of human community; our proud autonomy; and our idolatrous refusal to worship God.[30]

The cross of Christ is the perfect model for the twin attitudes of self-denial and self-affirmation. Christ's sacrifice affirms the value of our true self while at the same time nails to the cross one's own carnal desires.[31]

THE IMPORTANCE OF A HEALTHY SELF-ESTEEM

We came to the conclusion that a biblical view of self-esteem is one which recognizes that our value is because of what God did for us. He created us in His image, and Jesus sacrificed His life for us. Our attempt to defend self-esteem as a viable Christian belief is not an attempt to compromise the biblical data in order to pacify Christian psychologists. Rather, it is an earnest effort to be fair to all that the Bible says about ourselves. Actually, there are four reasons why we need to preserve a biblical view of self-esteem:

1. Self-esteem is important for the healthy functioning of a child.
2. Self-esteem is important for having a healthy outlook on life.
3. Self-esteem is important for proper relationships.
4. Self-esteem is important for having a proper view of God.

Self-esteem and the Healthy Functioning of a Child. Building a biblical perspective of self-esteem into the lives of our children is essential for child-rearing. Dobson has found that even a five-year-old is "capable of 'feeling' his own lack of worth."[32] Without a healthy sense of self-love and self-worth, a child will not have the confidence to try new things, explore the world around him, and engage in personal relationships. A practical book on this subject is Dr. Ross Campbell's *How to Really Love Your Child* where he urges us to build healthy self-concepts in our children through eye contact, physical contact, focused attention, and discipline.[33]

Self-Esteem and a Healthy Outlook on Life. This point goes hand in hand with the first. McDowell makes a good point:

> *Persons with a good, healthy sense of self-worth feel significant. . . . Such persons can interact with others and appreciate their worth too. They radiate hope, joy and trust. They are alive to their feelings. They accept themselves as delightful to God — a ship moving forward confidently, under full sail. They believe in themselves as lovable, worthy and competent parts of God's creation, sinful by nature, but redeemed and reconciled to God to become all He wants them to be.*[34]

On the other hand, "An inadequate self-image robs us of the energy and powers of attention to relate to others because we are absorbed with our own inadequacies."[35] Have you ever met people who are afraid to try anything new, like a new game or sport? These people are afraid to fail because their lack of self-esteem places their security within the confines of success. Therefore, they will never try anything unless they are certain that they can accomplish it successfully.

Self-Esteem and Proper Relationships. As discussed earlier, the command to love others as ourselves is based on a healthy self-love. People with poor self-images often berate themselves, hoping others will disagree and give them praise. Or sometimes they will try to establish their superiority by ridiculing others.[36]

Dobson talks about recent evidence which suggests that an inferiority-complex is "the major force behind the rampaging incidence of rape today." Many rapists are not after mere sexual satisfaction, which is fairly easy to come by in our society today. Evidence shows that they want to humiliate their victims. By lowering the dignity of others, they attempt to heighten theirs.[37]

Self-Esteem and a Proper View of God. Psychological studies indicate that self-esteem is important for having a proper view of God. Peter Benson and Bernard Spilka conducted a study of 128 teenagers who had the same religious training.[38] They discovered that those who had a positive self-esteem more readily accepted an image of God as loving and accepting. Those who had negative self-concepts tended to see God as vindictive and wrathful.[39] Sadly, those with poor self-concepts found it difficult to believe that God was loving and compassionate.

Christian psychologists Myron R. Chartier and Larry A. Goehner performed a similar study, which involved eighty-four tenth- and eleventh-graders from Western Christian High School in Glendora, California. This study yielded practically the same results as the Benson and Spilka investigation.

Chartier and Goehner also studied the students' relationships with their parents. They discovered that when a child received "a high degree of constructive, growth-producing communication from parents," he or she developed a high self-esteem. Low self-esteem was related to "receiving a high degree of destructive, growth-inhibiting communication from their parents."[40]

These studies indicate that an adolescent's view of God (God-esteem) and himself (self-esteem) is directly related to his or her family atmosphere. "How an adolescent feels about himself and about God may very well be influenced by the quality of the communicative relationship that has existed between himself and his parents."[41]

A balanced view of self-esteem is not only biblical, but practical as well. It is important for the normal functioning of a child. It affects our outlook on life as well as our relationships with others. And most importantly, a poor self-image may be detrimental to a proper view of God.

Notes

1. Dave Hunt, *Peace, Prosperity, and the Coming Holocaust* (Eugene, Oreg.: Harvest House, 1983), 178; also 248ff.
2. Douglas R. Groothuis, *Unmasking the New Age* (Downers Grove, Ill.: InterVarsity, 1986), 81.
3. Dave Hunt and T. A. McMahon, *The Seduction of Christianity* (Eugene, Oreg.: Harvest House, 1985), 193.
4. Ibid., 57.
5. Ibid., 155.
6. See also Gen. 6:5; Pss. 51:1; 58:3; Eph. 2:3; Rom. 3:10, 12, 18.
7. Paul C. Vitz, "Was Jesus Self-Actualized?" *New Covenant,* July 1980, 10.
8. David G. Myers, "The Inflated Self," *The Christian Century,* December 1982, 1226.
9. David G. Myers, *The Inflated Self* (New York: Seabury, 1980); cited in Groothuis, *Unmasking,* 86.
10. Charles R. Swindoll, *Improving Your Serve: The Art of Unselfish Living* (Waco, Tex.: Word, 1981), 39.
11. Hunt and McMahon, *Seduction,* 195.
12. Ibid.
13. Ibid.
14. R. C. Sproul, *The Holiness of God* (Wheaton, Ill.: Tyndale House, 1985), 49.
15. Hunt and McMahon, *Seduction,* 14; Dave Hunt, *Beyond Seduction* (Eugene, Oreg.: Harvest House, 1987), 175-176.
16. Hunt, *Beyond Seduction,* 177.
17. Josh McDowell, *His Image, My Image* (San Bernardino, Calif.: Here's Life, 1984), 34.
18. Ibid., 32.
19. Ibid., 106.
20. Hunt, *Beyond Seduction,* 174.
21. McDowell, *His Image,* 31.
22. Ibid., 33.
23. James Dobson, *Hide or Seek* (Old Tappan, N.J.: Revell, 1974), 156.
24. Lev. 19:18; Matt. 19:19; 22:39; Mark 12:31; Luke 10:27; Rom. 13:9.
25. McDowell, *His Image,* 37.
26. Rollo May, *Man's Search for Himself* (New York: Norton, 1953), 100; cited in McDowell, *His Image,* 32.
27. Hunt, *Beyond Seduction,* 181.
28. John W. Stott, "Am I Supposed to Love Myself or Hate Myself?" *Christianity Today,* 20 April 1984, 26-28.
29. Stott, 28.
30. Ibid.
31. Ibid.
32. Dobson, *Hide or Seek,* 7-8.
33. Ross Campbell, *How to Really Love Your Child* (Wheaton, Ill.: Victor, 1981).
34. McDowell, *His Image,* 20.
35. Ibid.
36. Ibid., 44.

37. Dobson, *Hide or Seek,* 154.
38. These subjects (average age: 15.4 years old) had parents who were Catholic, they considered themselves Catholic, they all attended Catholic high schools, they were members of a local parish for at least ten years, they had never been members of another denomination, they never associated with a non-Catholic religious organization, and they all had basically the same religious training. Every subject believed in God and regarded religion as being very important.
39. Peter Benson and Bernard Spilka, "God Image as a Function of Self-Esteem and Locus of Control," *Journal for the Scientific Study of Religion* 12 (September 1973):297-310. Also see Myron R. Chartier and Larry A. Goehner, "A Study of the Relationship of Parent-Adolescent Communication, Self-Esteem, and God Image," *Journal of Psychology and Theology* 4 (Summer 1976):227-232.
40. Myron R. Chartier and Larry A. Goehner, "A Study of the Relationship of Parent-Adolescent Communication, Self-Esteem, and God Image," *Journal of Psychology and Theology* 4 (Summer 1976):227.
41. Ibid., 230.

SIX
PLAGUE, PLACEBO, OR PURGE?
The Thorny Question of Inner Healing

Mary's desire for her husband John is just as great as John's desire for her. Yet something prevents her from getting as close to John as she would like. Something inside of Mary makes her cringe in repulsion and guilt whenever John approaches her. The door to intimacy is barricaded with threats and hurts from the past.

A counselor learns that Mary was sexually abused as a child by someone she respected, admired, and trusted. The tortured memory of her lost innocence is too much for Mary to bear. Sexual contact makes her bristle with fear and contempt. Her situation is worsened by the volatile mixture of love and repulsion for her husband.

Slowly reentering her painful past is no easy task. But the counselor skillfully guides Mary into picturing Jesus as a forgiving and protective shield between her and her abuser. And while the memory will probably not be erased, the hurt and guilt can be swept away. She now pictures herself forgiving her attacker and being comforted by the love of Christ. Scripture is read and a prayer of thanksgiving is offered for Mary's "inner healing."

WHAT IS INNER HEALING?
Even after conversion, a person is often plagued by emotional and mental problems. In recent years, the ministry of what is called "inner healing" has gained wide acceptance among Christians and non-Christians alike. Speakers, counselors, and authors like Agnes Sanford, Ruth Carter

Stapleton, John and Paula Sandford, Dennis and Rita Bennett, Francis and Judith MacNutt, Leanne Payne, and David Seamands have popularized the inner healing ministry. Such authors have published such widely read books as *Inner Healing through Healing of Memories, Forgiveness and Inner Healing, Transformation of the Inner Man, Healing the Wounded Spirit, How to Pray for Inner Healing for Yourself and Others,* and *Healing for Damaged Emotions.*

But what is inner healing? In contrast to external, physical healing, inner healing is the healing of the internal, immaterial aspect of man. Inner healing is "the healing of the inner man: the mind, the emotions, the painful memories, the dreams."[1]

Using prayer as the guiding tool in this ministry, inner healing claims to set us free from feelings of resentment, rejection, self-pity, depression, guilt, fear, and hatred. Inner healing is viewed as a kind of "spiritual surgery" where Jesus removes the emotionally and mentally crippling "growths that have entered the inner self."[2] Jesus heals the painful memories that can be the roadblocks to emotional and mental well-being. The memories will not be forgotten but the hurt is removed from them.[3]

The ministry of inner healing basically involves three steps. First, the counselor discovers the past event which caused the present problem. Second, the client visualizes the presence of Jesus taking care of the painful memory. Third, a prayer of thanksgiving is offered for the healing.

Inner healing therapy is primarily meant for believers. Ministers of inner healing want to help spiritual maturity and psychological well-being in the believer. "So many people become Christians—they're born again and filled with the Spirit. But they wonder, 'What do I do now?' They're missing the growth in sanctification, which is what inner healing brings," John Sandford says.[4] They believe that this ministry is a way of applying the grace and power of the conversion experience to the area of psychological need.

DOESN'T INNER HEALING INVOLVE THE OCCULT?

Some Christian writers have charged inner healing ministers with engaging in occult practices. Those who are involved in the ministry of inner healing readily admit that a central technique of this counseling therapy is visualization. However, they insist that they are not borrowing occult techniques.

According to Dave Hunt and T. A. McMahon's *The Seduction of Christianity*, occult visualization involves the belief that we can create or manipulate reality through mental processes.[5] Hunt claims that inner healing assumes that "to create one's own image in the imagination will therefore produce faith and healing."[6] But inner healing author David Seamands insists that mainline inner healing ministers do not believe that they are creating or manipulating reality in any way. Inner healers are often lumped together with what he calls the "far-out prosperity people" who "say that if your imagination is strong enough, it will create reality."[7]

For example, when the counselor asks the client to visualize Jesus being there, comforting her at the scene of the tragic event, he is not telling her to make up something that never took place. Jesus was there (Heb. 13:5). She just was not cognizant of his presence. Picturing Jesus with us assists us in understanding and applying what God's Word has already declared. And so, inner healers argue, the client did not create the reality of the Lord's presence; she simply realized the reality that was already true.

But what value is there in counseling a girl raped at the age of six to imagine that Jesus is holding, washing, and cleansing her? True, Jesus was there. But he never literally held her in his arms. Is this aspect of inner healing going too far?

Not necessarily. This kind of visualization need not be equated with Eastern mysticism and occultism. As long as the client realizes that she is not creating a physical Jesus who picked her up in his arms and that Jesus did not really pick her up when she was six years old, the image of his picking her up can be a helpful way of describing God's providential care for his creatures.

Betty Tapscott rightly makes the point that some form of visualization, at various levels of abstraction, occur in normal Christian activities such as in the singing of hymns.[8] For example, are we engaging in the occult or idolatry when we sing the song "Turn Your Eyes upon Jesus"? Who can read the parables of Jesus without visualizing the scenes to some extent? Even inner healing critic Don Matzat admits that "if while I am reading the story of Jesus walking on the water I envision the scene in my imagination as I continue to read the biblical account, I am properly using the God-given gift of imagination."[9]

Consider the helpful visualization in the well-known fictional story "Footprints."

There was a man who had just died, and he was reviewing the foot-steps that he had taken in his life. He looked down and noticed that all over the mountains and difficult places he had traveled, there was one set of footprints, but over the plains and down the hills there were two sets of footprints, as if someone had walked by his side. He turned to Jesus and said, "There is something I don't un-derstand . . . why is it that down the hills and over the smooth and easy places, you have walked by my side, but over the rough and difficult places I have walked alone, for I see in these areas there is just one set of footprints?" Jesus turned to the man and said, "It is true that while your life was easy I walked along your side, but here when the walking was hard and the paths were difficult, I real-ized that was the time you needed me most . . . and that is why I carried you.

The telling of that story portrays biblical truth in a way that evokes emo-tion, reflection, and a proper response to the character of God. This is why the Bible is not written in mere propositions, which can be cold, lifeless, and sterile. Scripture is the record of God's truths packaged in vivid, fleshed-out stories that command a response from the pictures they project. Inner healing can avoid occult influence by using the im-agination only to evoke those events or spiritual realities which really did occur (e.g., the ever-present God of comfort) rather than an attempt to materialize reality by their thoughts.

Dave Hunt tries to debunk the ministry of inner healing by arguing that "assorted occultists obtain equal results through visualizing all man-ner of 'inner guides.' "[10] However, in Matthew 7:22, Jesus told his dis-ciples that those who are out of the will of the Father claim to "perform many miracles." There are three Greek words—power (*dunamis*), sign (*semeion*), and wonder (*teras*)—used in reference to the miracles of Christ and the apostles (Acts 2:22; Heb. 2:4). It is significant that these are the same three words used of demonic works of power in 2 Thes-salonians 2:9, even though they are called "false wonders." Does this mean that the miracles of Jesus are suspect just because demons can coun-terfeit some of them? Of course not. The miracles of Moses were not invalidated simply because some of them were simulated by the magi-cians of Pharaoh (Exod. 7:10-12). Neither can a legitimate ministry of inner healing be invalidated by New Age sorcery. Such accusations rely more on guilt-by-association than on logic.

THE DANGER OF EXPERIENTIALISM

Some inner healers claim that although inner healing is not based on new or extrabiblical revelation, its use of visualization falls into the category of "a word of knowledge." [11] They believe that God discloses information needed for counseling—just as he would with a word of knowledge, except now this information is given visually rather than linguistically.

Even apart from the question of whether the special gift of healing is possessed by anyone today, we should take note of some inherent dangers in inner healing. [12] Even inner healer David Seamands admits that "There is always that danger [of demonic influence] in anything experiential. . . . Again and again we must always go back to Scripture. That's the blanket test. Test the spirits and discern the spirits." [13]

Seamands's point is that anything experiential should not be judged as being true or false simply because an experience occurred. Obviously, one could have a real experience of something false and unbiblical. Experience must be judged by the Scriptures, never the other way around.

Furthermore, the notion of receiving a picture directly from God is not an essential element in the ministry of inner healing. God is omnipresent—He is everywhere, so He is present at every event (Josh. 1:9; Ps. 139:7; Acts 17:27-28). We know that our God is a God of comfort and compassion (Exod. 34:6; Ps. 36:5; 1 John 4:16). Helpful images of his reassuring presence can be abstracted from truths in the Bible without recourse to so-called new "revelation." Thus, it is unnecessary to receive some extrabiblical "picture" of knowledge for an inner healing ministry. The Bible is sufficient for faith and practice.

IS INNER HEALING PSYCHOLOGICALLY VIABLE?

Even if inner healing was biblically allowable, does it work and is it safe? What does the field of psychology have to say about it? That is, is there evidence from psychological studies which confirm the validity of inner healing? Unfortunately, the verdict is not clear at present. The procedures and results of inner healers are not well-documented, and so very few clinical studies are available right now. However, there are some analyses of which we should be aware.

SOME POSITIVE CONTRIBUTIONS
OF INNER HEALING

First, the surfacing of the inner healing ministry is a marked improvement over the former outlook of many Christians towards psychological problems. As David Hazard of *Charisma* has written, "A decade ago life-controlling sins and weaknesses were chalked up to demon interference. A prayer of deliverance would follow."[14] So rather than treat every psychological illness with an exorcism, many charismatics now recognize the place of therapy and counseling.

Second, the ministry of inner healing focuses on forgiveness. The bottom line of inner healing is "either forgiving yourself or forgiving someone else."[15] Forgiveness is central in a healthy psyche as well as a very biblical concept (Matt. 18:21-35). The apostle John said that confessing our sins and receiving forgiveness from God was the only way the word could have a place in our lives (1 John 1:9).

Third, inner healing also involves visualizing the reality of Jesus Christ being present in the tragic event which helped cause our present psychological problem. One psychologist noted that "The introduction of a good person ([a] pleasant stimulus) into a traumatic experience ([an] unpleasant stimulus) should provide an element of desensitization" to the tragic memory.[16]

This act of visualization, as we said earlier, is a way of appropriating the grace and power which trusting Christ brought into our lives. It is a way of helping the believer by making the fact of being a renewed creature an experienced reality.

SOME CONCERNS ABOUT INNER HEALING

However, there are also some reasons for caution in the area of inner healing. First, there seems to be an overemphasis on past events as simplistic causes of current problems. Christian psychiatrist Basil Jackson has written, "The past is only one aspect of emotional difficulties." There are "many conflicts [that] existentially lie in the present and even more are related to the individual's notion of the future." Jackson also urges us to understand that clients often falsify and fabricate "what he feels the healer is searching for."[17]

Second, releasing formerly repressed memories can be dangerous. Even advocates of inner healing admit that the unleashing of repressed memories is potentially dangerous to the psychological health of the client. "There is the possibility of ego fragmentation rather than integration for people with poor ego strength."[18] Inner healers, untrained in such management of psychological trauma, could find themselves in situations beyond their expertise and experience.

Third, the use of visualization has much in common with hypnotherapy techniques in that it involves a form of "mind control" in order to alleviate a particular psychological ailment. Not that all forms of using our mind to influence our body are necessarily bad. We often use our minds to control feelings of nervousness and anxiety. Many cases of sickness are discovered to be psychosomatic and, therefore, often "curable" through mental control.

However, studies on forms of mind control such as biofeedback have resulted in what is called symptom substitution. The Diamond Headache Clinic in Chicago conducted a study which discovered that of those migraine patients who had learned to control headaches through biofeedback, two-thirds reported the development of new psychosomatic symptoms within five years.[19]

The final verdict is not yet in on inner healing from a psychological point of view. But the evidence thus far warrants caution.

IS A BIBLICAL PSYCHOLOGY A CONTRADICTION OF TERMS?

In response to critics, inner healers such as Betty Tapscott, Rita Bennett, David Seamands, and John and Paula Sandford argue that there is biblical justification for inner healing. Passages such as Psalm 147:3 point out that the Lord wants to "heal the brokenhearted." The writer of Hebrews warned believers to make sure that there was "no root of bitterness to grow up to cause trouble and defile many" (Heb. 12:15). And while Romans 12:2, "Be transformed by the renewing of your mind," should not be narrowed to our twentieth-century understanding of psychological well-being, renewing of the mind must certainly include psychological health.

We could also point out the many verses inner healers use out of context and with a poor understanding of what the biblical words meant in their cultural situation, but surely we must admit that the Bible recognizes that we have inner, psychological problems that are in need of "healing." Seamands responds correctly to the criticisms that if inner healing "is biblical in the literal sense," then we should be able to "find it in Scripture."

If we apply that reasoning to everything, we might as well all join the Amish and wear clothes without buttons, or we might as well refuse penicillin to a sick child. We don't find those practices in the Bible either. The basic question then is not whether we find visualization literally in the Bible. The question is whether visualization is consistent with the principles stated in Scripture. [20]

Ras Robinson, writing in *Fulness* magazine, emphasized that "it is of utmost importance to keep the inner healing process biblical. We must refuse to become involved in fad methods." [21] Martin Lynch, who along with his wife, Sally, is an advocate of inner healing as well as a founder and executive director of the Association of Christian Therapists, says, "All theories of secular psychology assume that there is no God. So what's missing are the two basic elements of repentance and forgiveness." [22]

The biblical concepts of forgiveness and repentance are two essential elements in a Christian psychology that protect us from temptations for self-exaltation and self-deification. The inner healing ministry of forgiveness assumes that people need to own up to their sins and failures. Says John Sandford,

> *Sometimes people who think they're practicing inner healing are really allowing someone to have a 'pity party.' At times, these counselors bring comfort when they should be confronting (the subject), encouraging him to bring his sin to the cross.*
>
> *Look at Colossians 3, where Paul says that we should not lie to one another but put off the old nature with its practices. An untrained counselor will hear a confession but not deal with the sinful process of living that developed because of past hurts. It's putting Band-Aids over gaping wounds.* [23]

Despite accusations, not all inner healers confuse Christian psychology with the work of grace. They believe that "true healing and cleansing can come only through Christ and His atoning work and the work of the Spirit in the believer." Inner healing is not viewed by its Christian supporters as some kind of a cure-all. They are merely defending it as a viable form of Christian therapy. [24]

Critics of inner healing often are guilty of throwing out the baby with the bath water. John Sandford himself recognizes the inconsistencies that have been made among inner healers and at least claims to welcome the corrections. But he cautions us against rejecting the whole concept. [25]

In *Beyond Seduction*, Dave Hunt makes explicit his reasons for rejecting the possibility of a Christian psychology. The following is a list of his objections and our responses.

1. Psychology was founded by anti-Christians and is therefore anti-biblical.[26] Hunt's reasoning here is that since psychology was first introduced by humanists and occultists, it therefore follows that psychology must be humanistic or occultic.[27] He uses 1 Corinthians 2:14 to support his thesis: "A natural man [unbeliever] does not accept the things of the Spirit of God; for they are foolishness to him, and he cannot understand them, because they are spiritually appraised."

In response, it should be noted that the context of this passage makes it clear that those "things of the Spirit," which seem "foolish" to unbelievers are not psychological ailments like depression, paranoia, neuroses, etc. "The word of the cross is to those who are perishing foolishness" (1 Cor. 1:18). In other words, the unbeliever does not accept the sacrificial death of Christ for his salvation because it seems foolish to him.

Hunt commits what is called "the genetic fallacy" in logic by trying to denigrate truth claims because of their source. But the demons (not a very Christian source of truth!) were the first to recognize Jesus as the Messiah. James tells us that the demons know that God is one (James 2:19). Truth can come from an anti-Christian source. Many modern day inventions and discoveries we take for granted came from godless thinkers.

For example, the inventor of the alternating current motor, Nicolai Tesla, got the idea from a vision while reading a pantheistic poet! And Friedrich August Kekule's model for the benzene molecule came from a vision he had of a snake biting its tail.[28] This does not make their inventions or discoveries any less true or workable. Truth is available to non-Christians as well as Christians.

2. Psychology is a religion and is therefore in conflict with Christianity.[29] Hunt tries to equate the "things of the Spirit of God" with the realm of psychology in order to prove that unbelievers are ignorant of "psychological" problems. He does this by cleverly defining Christian psychology out of existence. "There is no such thing as a mental illness," he writes, "it is either a physical problem in the brain (such as a chemical imbalance or nutritional deficiency) or it is a moral or spiritual problem."[30] Hunt concludes that since psychology has nothing to do with physical science and there is no such thing as a mental science, "psychology can only claim to be a spiritual science. But this is an impossible contradiction of terms. Psychology is a religion trying to pass itself off as a science."[31]

This simplistic model of the nature of man is meant to deal the death blow to Christian psychology. But Christian philosophers have debated for centuries over the relationship between the mind and the body. No less controversial is the age-old debate among theologians over man's soul, spirit, and body. The fact is, the only point of general agreement among theologians is that the Bible teaches a soul-body unity that we have yet to completely fathom. The physical and spiritual dimensions of man cannot so easily be compartmentalized and dissected. And the mental aspect of man cannot be defined away.

Also, if there is no such thing as a mental state, then everything we used to relegate to the mental arena is in reality spiritual. Does this mean that depression, for example, is purely a spiritual problem? Then why are there unbelievers who hardly ever have a bout with depression while there are committed believers who daily battle depression? How does Hunt's theory explain the mental anguish that often plagues a rape victim? Her spiritual state had nothing to do with her victimization and subsequent problems. It does no good for Hunt to argue here that if she only places her trust in the Word of God then she will be healed. For the fact that physical problems are sometimes healed through spiritual answers does not mean that the problem was any less physical. Likewise, the fact that psychological problems are sometimes healed through spiritual means doesn't make the problem less psychological.

3. Allowing a Christian psychology would be tantamount to saying that the Bible needs help. Such an admission would denigrate the veracity of Scripture. While Hunt admits that "the Bible doesn't claim to cover every subject,"[32] he says that "the Bible claims to offer the only and complete truth."[33] But numerous passages such as Psalm 19:1 and Romans 1:20 and 2:12-14 tell us that God has also revealed truth outside of the Bible. This is called general revelation. And if Hunt is going to grant that "not everything in psychology is anti-Christian" then how would it would be "dishonoring to God and a denial of the sufficiency of the gospel and of Scripture" to consider sources outside the Bible to either "support or supplement our Christian faith"?[34]

Further, even granting Hunt's mistaken view that God has not revealed Himself outside the Bible, he poses a false dilemma. Hunt unfairly stacks the deck against Christian psychology. His argument is basically this: Psychology either opposes the Bible or supplements it. If it opposes the Bible, then it is clearly wrong. If it supplements the Bible, then it maligns the adequacy of Scripture. Of course, he ignores the option that the findings of psychology could help bring better understanding as to how biblical principles are applied.

We often legitimately use extra-biblical sources (commentaries, linguistic studies, archaeological discoveries, historical records, scientific data, etc.) to get a better handle on the meaning of the Bible for the original audience so that we can better apply it to today's audience. Indeed, the Bibles we read in English are in part the product of such tools, some of which were researched and written by unbelievers!

For example, Christian psychologists Paul Meier and Frank Minirth discovered that "pent-up anger is the root of nearly all clinical depression."[35] This piece of data offers valuable insight into the command "Be angry and yet do not sin; do not let the sun go down on your anger" (Eph. 4:26). Anger should not be repressed to a boiling point and must be resolved before the day is out. "Repressing anger often leads to displacing it on something or someone else. Unconscious grudges held inside can lead to physical symptoms such as insomnia, fatigue, or loss of appetite."[36] The information and medicines available today provide a progressive way to treat this mental illness in a way that couldn't be treated in the first century just as there was no vaccine for polio or tuberculosis either.

Seamands hits the nail squarely on the head when he says, "Some of the criticism comes from an inadequate philosophy of knowledge."

> *Christians have been grateful for every new truth such as the polio vaccine. Calvinists have believed in common grace, Wesleyans in prevenient grace. The Roman Catholics have the concept of natural theology or general revelation. All truth is God's truth, wherever you find it.*[37]

To say that all truth is God's truth is to say that all truth has its ultimate source in God and that God would confirm it as true.[38] Historic Christianity has believed that the Scriptures are not as an exhaustive revelation of everything man can know but rather a sufficient revelation of everything he needs to know for faith and conduct. It is clearly within orthodox Christianity to affirm that non-Christians as well as Christians perceive truth, if only partially. All truth is God's truth, no matter where it is found or by whom it is discovered.

Secular psychologies contain a mixture of error and truth. It is our job as responsible, thinking Christians to sift the truth from the errors and incorporate these truths into our systematic body of knowledge (2 Cor. 10:5). There is no such thing as secular truth and Christian truth. There is only truth and error.

We should not reject psychology in total and deny the truths discovered in the field. As noted earlier, God reveals truth through general revelation too. Rather, we must steer a middle course between exalting the field of psychology and rejecting its findings completely.

In conclusion, inner healing is a viable counseling ministry if it is used cautiously, moderately, and keeps the use of imagination within the bounds of the principles and promises discovered in Scripture. The traps of "new age occultism" can be avoided if inner healers do not cross the line into reality-manipulation and self-deification. Legitimate inner healing can be contrasted with illegitimate inner healing in the following ways:

	INNER HEALING	
	LEGITIMATE	ILLEGITIMATE
Key technique	Imagination	Visualization
Presence of Jesus	Realized	Manufactured
Use of psychology	To apply Bible	To replace it
Relation to reality	Adjust to it	Manipulate it

Notes

1. Don Turner, "Is Inner Healing a Valid Ministry?" *Fulness*, March-April 1986, 17.
2. Ibid.
3. Ras Robinson, "Inner Healing," *Fulness*, March-April 1986, 42.
4. Quoted in David Hazard, "An Inside Look at Inner Healing," *Charisma*, September 1986, 48.
5. Dave Hunt and T. A. McMahon, *The Seduction of Christianity* (Eugene, Oreg.: Harvest House, 1985), 123, 173.
6. Dave Hunt, *Beyond Seduction* (Eugene, Oreg.: Harvest House, 1987), 211.
7. Turner, "Inner Healing," 20.
8. Ibid.
9. Don Matzat, *Inner Healing: Deliverance or Deception?* (Eugene, Oreg.: Harvest House, 1987), 62-63.
10. Hunt, *Beyond Seduction*, 205.
11. Turner, "Inner Healing," 18, 20.
12. It should be noted here that the authors do not believe that the Scriptures advocate that the gifts of the Spirit are still operational (as gifts) today. For more information see Norman L. Geisler, *Christian Apologetics* (Grand Rapids: Baker, 1976), chapter 18; Norman L. Geisler and William Nix, *General Introduction to the Bible*, rev. ed. (Chicago: Moody, 1986), chapters 6 and 16; and Nor-

man L. Geisler, *Signs and Wonders* (Wheaton, III.: Tyndale House, 1988), appendix 8.

13. Turner, "Inner Healing," 22.
14. Hazard, "Inside Look," 44.
15. Ibid., 46.
16. Leonard J. Cerny II, "Reaction to a Critique of Ruth Carter Stapleton's Ministry of 'Inner Healing,' " *Journal of Psychology and Theology* 8 (Fall 1980):202.
17. Basil Jackson, "Stapleton: A Study in Psychotheological Naivete," *Journal of Psychology and Theology* 8 (Fall 1980):195-196.
18. Cerny, "Reaction to a Critique," 202.
19. Nathan Szajnberg and Seymour Diamond, "Biofeedback, Migraine Headache and New Symptom Formation," *Headache Journal* 20:29-31.
20. Turner, "Inner Healing," 21.
21. Robinson, "Inner Healing," 42.
22. Hazard, "Inside Look," 48.
23. Ibid.
24. Turner, "Inner Healing," 19, 21.
25. Ibid., 22.
26. Hunt, *Beyond Seduction,* 138-139, 172.
27. Don Matzat echoes the same argument in *Inner Healing: Deliverance or Deception?* cited earlier.
28. See Ian Barbour, *Issues in Science and Religion* (Englewood Cliffs, N.J.: Prentice-Hall, 1986), 158.
29. Hunt, *Beyond Seduction,* 110.
30. Ibid., 127.
31. Ibid.
32. Ibid., 125.
33. Ibid., 126.
34. Ibid., 110.
35. Paul D. Meier, Frank B. Minirth, and Frank B. Wichern, *Introduction to Psychology and Counseling: Christian Perspectives and Applications* (Grand Rapids: Baker, 1982), 261.
36. Ibid.
37. Turner, "Inner Healing," 19.
38. It does not mean everything someone considers true is really true. Matzat echoes Hunt's rejection of the "all truth is God's truth" position (*Inner Healing,* 35-36, 38-39).

SEVEN
BUT IS IT HEALTHY?
The Hope of Holistic Health

I died last night. I still remember the taunting chants of the village vodunist: "I will turn you into one of the undead!" he screamed over and over in his native tongue. Threats like these were common during my stay in Haiti, but this time was different. His eyes pierced my soul like an ice pick jammed between my ribs. A cold chill shot through my spine. In my last glimpse of him before I passed out was the blurred vision of his sinister smile.

When I awoke, my friends were wailing in distress as the village physician pronounced me dead! But I'm not dead yet. I couldn't be. I can still think . . . hear! I tried to speak, but my lips wouldn't move. Those fools covered me with earth and left me for dead! My mind is screaming, "I'm alive, I'm alive!" but no one hears me.

Seven days have passed and I still have tingling sensations all over my body, like millions of ants crawling under my skin. My eyes feel as though someone has stretched the lids apart with tweezers and pinned them to my forehead and cheeks. My lips are thick and pasty, I cannot swallow, and saliva flows from my mouth. Large, bulbous blisters have formed, and my skin is flaking away. Have I truly become one of the living dead? A zombie? Someone please help me.

The above is a fictional account based on real occurrences. There is documented evidence of cursed people who have been declared dead, then buried for several days, only to rise again in a trancelike state. Does

77

the vodunist—the witch doctor—truly possess magical powers as he claims? What are we to make of it?

Recent research has demonstrated that the cause of the voodoo-zombie mystery is far from magical.[1] There is, in fact, a scientific explanation for the "undead." The vodunist mixes a concoction of various toxins from plants, snakes, tarantulas, millipedes, and blowfishes. Tetrodotoxin, a nerve toxin from the blowfish or puffer fish, has been found to be 160,000 times more potent than cocaine and over 500 times stronger than cyanide. A fatal dose of this toxin in a pure state could rest on the head of a pin.

The symptoms of tetrodotoxin are those of the so-called undead. It can induce paralysis and lower a person's heartbeat and metabolism to such a degree that even a trained physician might not discern the boundary between life and death.

At the proper time, the vodunist administers a paste, called *bokor,* that supposedly brings the buried "dead to life." However, research reveals that this "antidote" contains a potent psychoactive drug which brings on a state of disorientation and amnesia. If the tetrodotoxin and antidote paste have been mixed and applied correctly, everyone will think that the vodunist made a zombie.

We can apply the same reasoning to much of the holistic health movement. First we will briefly define holistic health and then present a correlation between the zombies of Haiti and this increasingly popular movement in the medical field.

WHAT IS HOLISTIC HEALTH?

Holistic health is often associated with the New Age movement because many of the concepts are compatible with New Age thinking.[2] Holistic medicine desires to treat the person as a whole being. Holistic healers refuse to limit their preventative and curative efforts to the body alone. Their practices treat the whole person as a body, mind, and spirit unity. Acupuncture, chiropractic, herbal medicine, biofeedback, yoga, shiatsu, rolfing, iridology, and homeopathy are all considered to be legitimate forms of holistic medicine. Describing and critiquing every holistic practice is beyond the realm of this chapter, but here are some common elements that make certain practices holistic:

1. A human being is more than just a conglomeration of physical matter. We are body-mind-spirit beings. Therefore, any lasting treatment must take into account this essential unity. For example, stress (a "mind" thing) can often bring about ulcers (a "body" thing). Physical conditions such as obesity can lead to depression.

2. Healing through natural means is always better than drugs and surgery. Thus, the use of massage techniques and/or use of herbs is preferred over prescription drugs.

3. We should be active participants in the healing process. Holistic health practitioners are against the conventional view of patient-as-passive-pincushion. Through the use of our knowledge and willpower, and for some, even psychic power, we can overcome our ailments.

4. Many holistic health practitioners go beyond the body-mind-spirit model to the body-universal-spirit model. In other words, we can be whole through getting in touch with the universal energy force (i.e., God) within us all.

HOLISTIC HEALTH FROM A BIBLICAL PERSPECTIVE

Many holistic health practices are not inherently New Age. That is, the mechanics of these practices are physiologically explainable and therefore need not be tied to a New Age worldview. Therefore, it would be unfair and unwise to reject holistic health simply because of its close association with the New Age. We must evaluate holistic medicine on its own merits.

● Either holistic health practices work (bring about the desired and predicted result) or they do not.

● If they do not work, then this demonstrates that their claims (e.g., New Age "sorcery" is the cause of the healing process) are false.

● On the other hand, if any of these practices work, then either it is the result of "magical" (such as those claimed by many New Age proponents) or natural (physiologically explainable) causes.

● "Magic" (i.e., tapping into the power or spirit of the universe) is not the correct explanation of how these holistic health practices work.[3]

There is no legitimate proof or evidence that magic is the correct explanation of how these practices work. Furthermore, just because someone says that magic will bring about a desired result and that result occurs does not necessarily mean that magic was indeed the cause (remember the vodunist). It may be that he does not know what he's talking about! He may not understand how a certain practice works thereby attributing the wrong cause to the right effect. And there are scientifically demonstrable evidences for naturalistic explanations.

● Therefore, there are natural causes for the results of the holistic health practices that work.[4]

The Support for Our Arguments. In order for our preceding argument to be valid, the following claims must be supported:

Some holistic health practices work. While there undoubtedly are some holistic health theories that range from the "inventive" to the bizarre, many techniques have a scientific basis. For example, even though most of the universal claims of acupuncture are greatly exaggerated, acupuncture can be very effective in many areas. Dr. John Bonica, chairman of both the department of anesthesiology at the University of Washington and the Ad Hoc Committee of Acupuncture of the National Institutes of Health, observed the use of acupuncture anesthesia in China.[5] Bonica statistically calculated that acupuncture is used less than 10 percent of the time. And since acupuncture cannot totally eliminate pain and discomfort, nearly every patient receives additional narcotic or barbiturate injections prior to or during surgery. In reality, only about 6 percent of the patients did not require significant supplemental medication.

Limitations aside, many operations have been performed with patients awake and alert. This provides a definite advantage in certain types of surgery. For example, a tragic cut of the larynx nerve in thyroid surgery can be avoided by monitoring the alert patient's voice normality. The successful use of acupuncture also minimizes problems with anesthesia while greatly reducing the cost of operations.

Biofeedback also serves many useful functions.[6] Through the use of special electronic equipment, biofeedback helps the individual control body functions that normally operate unconsciously. The theory is to deal with health problems volitionally by learning how skin temperature, pulse rate, and brain waves correspond to differing mental states.

As with acupuncture, biofeedback is not a cure-all. But despite its limitations, it has been useful in dealing with the management of severe headaches. Reading the contractions of head and neck muscles through special sensors, patients can learn to relax the pertinent areas of tension-causing muscle contractions.

Christian physicians and authors Paul Reisser, Teri Reisser, and John Weldon admit,

> *One would be hard-pressed to find fault with the use of biofeed-back for this type of application. The physiology involved is rela-*

tively straightforward, and there is no underlying metaphysical message which must be swallowed for the technique to work.[7]

Much could also be said about the benefits of herbs and natural food products. The point is, some holistic health practices work. But should we attribute this success to New Age-type causes?

Some New Agers claim that many forms of holistic health owe their results to the power of the New Age. The power of the New Age is the alleged god-force within us all that pervades all the universe.

Guru Saraswati described part of his sexual yogic rituals this way: "I experience the All as myself, the whole universe, desire and compassion. 'I am all that.' I contain all contradictions."[8] Another writer outlined the culmination of the yogic process:

> *Finally, he [the practicioner of yoga] is given the name and details of his own personal deity . . . generally a particular facet, or personified power aspect of one of the major deities of the sect. . . . The chela now has a formula for repetition, a ritual for practice, and a deity for personal worship.*[9]

Transcendental Meditation guru Maharishi Mahesh Yogi claimed that his disciples, "chanting to produce an effect in some other world, draw the attention of those higher beings or gods living there."[10]

Chiropractor John Thie, author of the popular *Touch for Health*, pictures his work as one of balancing and unblocking energies in the individual. He explains that these energies

> *are the energies of the universe, taking form in the individual. To really understand this, we must remember that we are all one with the universe, with the universal energy. When this energy is highly concentrated, we call it "matter," and our bodies are that matter. Therefore, our bodies are literally this universal energy, in some of its various forms.*[11]

With this worldview, it's no surprise that Thie's chiropractic techniques even include waving one's hands within two inches of the skin. In other words, the hands never touch the body! Certainly such a practice seems more akin to magic than to any kind of respectable medical procedure.

Much of holistic medicine does not require a background of New Age pantheism, but there can be no doubt that a good portion of the holistic health movement has wholeheartedly embraced an Eastern worldview.

The source of a practice does not determine whether it is good or bad—true or false? Earlier in this book, we argued that you cannot legitimately discount a truth claim just because of its source. As we noted, the demons were the first to recognize Jesus as Messiah publicly, and Jesus himself even said that sinful human fathers could be sources of good things. This principle also applies to the area of health.

When you get your eyes checked by an ophthalmologist, he administers a couple of drops of atropine in order to dilate your pupils. But did you know that his drug comes from the deadly belladonna, which in the Middle Ages was known as the "witches' herb"? It would be foolish to conclude that because the source of this drug was once occultically labeled, the drug itself is occult. (Nor does this make ophthalmologists satanic!)

Primitive sorcery is in fact a primary source for many of our modern medical practices. Many herbs are presently used in the form of medicines—digitalis, quinine, morphine, opium, hashish, hemp, coca, cinchona, eucalyptus, sarsaparilla, acacia, kousso, copaiba, guaiac, jalap, podophyllin, and quassia, just to name a few. They were all at one time believed to contain "spirits" which battled against the spirit of the disease.[12] Drugs used in ancient times were thought to attract good gods and repel the evil ones.[13] Even everyday accepted medical procedures such as isolation of the sick, special diets, and sanitary precautions were executed in a world engulfed by chants, spells, rituals, and dances.[14] Trephination, the ancient practice of practically boring a hole in the skull in order to treat convulsions, epilepsy, insanity, and injuries to the head, was originally intended to release the demonic spirit responsible for the ailment. But in 1953 this act, previously regarded as barbaric and uneducated, was discovered to have a physiological basis by three prominent neurosurgeons.[15]

Biblical scholars confirm that the ancient Sumerians from the latter part of the third millennium B.C. (definitely not Yahweh-worshipers!) were the forefathers of modern pharmacology.[16] Dr. Milton Carelton states,

> *Limited by what plant material could be grown in a given locality, wrapped in superstition and often based on false premises, out of this primitive folklore came the beginnings of pharmacology and medicine as we know them today.[17]*

We would be foolish to empty our medicine cabinets just because pharmacology has its roots in sorcery. The "sorcerers of old" did not realize that they were simply concocting chemicals that would work regardless of their attendant incantations. Now we can benefit from their genius without buying into their ignorance. This may also prove to be the case with some of modern holistic medicine.

The workings of holistic health can be explained without recourse to "magic" or the "god-force" or the "power within."[18] Many holistic health practices have a scientific foundation. As an example, even though more research is needed in the area of acupuncture, the studies thus far indicate a naturalistic explanation for its frequent success. The following is a summary of the findings presented in Reisser, Reisser, and Weldon's *New Age Medicine*:[19]

First, intense stimulation of one part of the body can decrease the sensations in another. Called *counterirritation,* this extremely old technique has been verified experimentally. Sometimes the application of a painfully cold stimulus to the leg, for example, has been found to decrease the perception of pain caused by electrical stimulation of the teeth.

Second, *referred pain,* which is pain experienced in a location that is removed from the true problem area, might explain why needling in one area of the body can affect another area.

Third, *trigger points* are highly sensitive areas that are usually distanced from the real injury point and often associated with muscle or joint pain. Stimulation of these trigger points, particularly with local anesthetic, can result in pain relief. Dr. Ronald Melzack of McGill University discovered an over 70 percent correlation between trigger points and acupuncture points.

Fourth, Melzack and fellow researcher P. D. Wall structured the *gate control* theory of pain based on verified neurological pathways. We once assumed that pain is transmitted directly to the brain like one phone connection to another. However, Melzack and Wall have proposed that a gate-like mechanism in the central nervous system opens and closes in varying degrees, altering the course of the pain sensation to the brain. Thus, the degree of experienced pain is affected by the indirectness of the pain transmission's route to the brain.

One way to hinder the directness of the pain transmission is to stimulate individual nerve fibers. The body's surface contains both large and small nerve fibers. Sensations travel through both kinds of fibers, but the small fibers transmit the bulk of the pain messages. Stimulation of the large fibers may "close the gate" and thus shut down or divert the messages from small fibers. Acupuncture possibly provides the necessary stimulation.

Fifth, current research at the National Institute of Mental Health reveals that the body may manufacture morphinelike substances (endorphins) under certain kinds of stimulation. It could be that while acupuncture avoids the use of external chemicals, it activates the body's own internal, natural anesthetic in response to the needles.[20]

In connection with all this, we should here mention another practice associated with the holistic sciences, the self-defense exercises known as the martial arts. The power to break bricks, granite, and blocks of ice have become a carnival standard. How does the karate expert drive a nail through a solid piece of wood with his forehead? The answer given is the power of *ki*. But what is *ki*? Is it a New Age force, as many contend?

Actually, even hard-core practitioners accept the fact that the ancients stumbled upon breathing techniques and kinetic exercises which are physiologically sound. Breaking bricks is a matter of speed, leverage, skill, and concentration. Aikido master Thomas H. Makiyama says that "anyone can learn aikido techniques if diligent practice is embarked upon on a regular basis—no supernatural source of strength is involved." After explaining how leverage, relaxation, and diversion of the opponent's force accounts for the success of the aikido expert, Makiyama concludes that it is a simple matter of "elementary physics."[21]

Like the zombie story that opened this chapter, many claims of "magic" have been found to be scientifically explainable. No magic was involved, just experimentally verifiable chemistry and physiology.

THE ISSUE: CHRISTIAN INVOLVEMENT IN HOLISTIC HEALTH

A thorough evaluation of every holistic health technique available today is beyond the scope of this chapter. However, the logic of our approach can be used to determine your involvement in any particular holistic health technique. Here are the guiding principles and steps that can be derived from the argument we have just presented:

1. **Determine whether or not the practice is inherently unbiblical.** For example, even though many occultists use acupuncture, it does not follow that acupuncture is an occult technique. Many occultists also brush their teeth, but this does not make dental hygiene satanic. The real

question is, Does the practice involve immorality (e.g., orgies, human sacrifice), idolatry (worship of anyone or anything other than the God of the Bible), or contact with demonic forces (e.g., spiritism, mediums, channelers)?

2. Will the practice lead anyone else into sin? That is, will it cause someone who has been part of this practice in an occult context to sin? If so, then just like the meat offered to idols in the New Testament, we should refuse to participate (see Rom. 14; 1 Cor. 8).

3. If the practice is acceptable within a biblical worldview, then find out if it really works. For example, read the literature on acupuncture, visit your local library and study the latest medical research on the practice, and consult a medical doctor that you trust. If everything checks out so that the practice looks worthwhile and conventional means have been exhausted, find a certified and reliable practitioner.

4. If the practice is biblically acceptable and scientifically feasible, make sure that the practitioner will not influence you with an unbiblical worldview. Does the karate instructor only teach athletic skill and good sportsmanship, or does he also espouse Zen sayings, read from Confucius, teach about magical powers, or involve his students in Eastern rituals? Evaluate the practitioner by his words and actions, not by his claims or label. In other words, there may be a Christian karate instructor who has unwittingly bought into Eastern mysticism. Conversely, there may be an unbelieving yoga teacher who only teaches the physiology of breathing, stretching, and relaxation without any overtones of Hindu thought.

SUMMARY

1. Some holistic health practices actually work—that is, they bring about the desired and predicted results.
2. All of these results can be explained naturalistically without recourse to "magical" sources.
3. Just because a practice has its roots in ancient occultism or sorcery does not necessarily make it an occult or New Age practice.
4. Christians should beware of getting involved in practices that are attended by practitioners who espouse nonbiblical worldviews.

Notes

1. See Wade Davis, *The Serpent and the Rainbow* (New York: Warner Books, 1985).
2. For a detailed evaluation of holistic health from a Christian perspective, see Paul C. Reisser, Teri K. Reisser, and John Weldon, *New Age Medicine: A Christian Perspective on Holistic Health* (Downers Grove, Ill.: InterVarsity, 1987).
3. There may be cases where supernatural power is a real cause of "holistic healing." However, the authors believe such cases to be based in evil supernatural powers. See chap. 3, on New Age occultism.
4. A more thorough form of this argument would include the God of the Bible and demons as possible supernatural sources of the results of holistic medicine:
   a. The successful result of holistic medicine is either due to supernaturalistic or naturalistic causes.

   A supernaturalistic cause could be one of three options: the New Age power that resides within the individual (that is, the god-force that pervades all the universe), the God of the Bible, or demonic power.

   A naturalistic cause would be something physiological—e.g., in the case of yoga, the deliberate breathing and concentration techniques help the individual achieve a relaxed state, not some mystical energy force in the universe bonding with the individual's spirit.
   b. The successful results of holistic medicine are not due to a supernatural cause.

   There is no evidence for this New Age power, and in fact such a power (pantheism) can be demonstrated to be false (see chap. 2).

   The God of the Bible does not act in a fashion that is compatible with this pantheistic concept. Theism is incompatible with pantheism (see chap. 2).

   In some cases, demonic power may lie behind the results of holistic medicine. However, it should be pointed out that even demonism is part of the theistic worldview and not of pantheism. Furthermore, the success of many New Age practices, as elaborated in this chapter, can be explained without recourse to the supernatural at all.
   c. Therefore, the successful results of holistic medicine are due to naturalistic causes. In this chapter, we have offered many examples of these scientific explanations.
5. Reisser, Reisser, and Weldon, *New Age Medicine,* 67-68.
6. Ibid., 135-136.
7. Reisser, Reisser, and Weldon also warn us of the New Age trappings that often accompany biofeedback. "Biofeedback has been used as a sort of 'electronic yoga,' a high tech means for altering consciousness and inducing psychic experiences" (136).
8. Swami Janakananda Saraswati, *Yoga, Tantra, and Meditation in Daily Life,* trans. Sheila Le Farge (London: Rider, 1975), 79.
9. B. Walker, *Tantrism: Its Secret Principles and Practices* (Wellingborough, England: Aquarian, 1982), 27, as quoted in Brooks Alexander's "Tantra: The Worship and Occult Power of Sex," *SCP Newsletter* 11 (Summer 1985):8.

10. Maharishi Mahesh Yogi, *Meditations of Maharishi Mahesh Yogi* (New York: Bantam, 1968), 17-18.

11. John Thie, *Touch for Health* (Marina del Rey, Calif.: DeVorss, 1973).

12. R. Schoental, "Herbal Medicines and Disease," *Journal of Tropical Pediatrics* 3 (March 1957): 208, and H. H. Walser and H. M. Koelbing, eds., *Medicine and Ethnology* (Baltimore: The Johns Hopkins Press, 1971), 128.

13. A. Rosalie David, *The Ancient Egyptians* (London: Routledge & Kegan Paul, 1982), 142.

14. Walser and Koelbing, *Medicine and Ethnology,* 128.

15. Michael M. Rytel, "Trephinations in Ancient Peru," *Polish Medical Science and History Bulletin* 5 (January 1962):42-43; Judson Duland, "Depressed Fracture and Trephining of the Skull by the Incas of Peru," *Annals of Medical History* 7 (November 1937):553. See also Ralph Gower, *The New Manners and Customs of Bible Times* (Chicago: Moody, 1987), 171.

16. Edward M. Blaiklock and R. K. Harrison, *The New International Dictionary of Biblical Archaeology* (Grand Rapids: Zondervan, 1983), 307; Gower, *Manners and Customs,* 171; Sir E. A. Wallis Budge, *Herb Doctors and Physicians in the Ancient World: The Divine Origin of the Craft of the Herbalist* (Chicago: Ares, 1978). "Nevertheless, sufficient evidence remains to confirm that later medical systems in Europe and the Near East derived their principles from Egypt, for it was here that, despite the continued use of magic as an alternative method, the basis of a medical science and profession was established (David, *The Ancient Egyptians,* 143).

17. Dr. Milton Carelton, "Herbs: Their Ancient Influences on Mankind," *Today's Health,* March 1964, 33.

18. We are essentially arguing that much of holistic health should not be understood under a New Age umbrella because there are naturalistic explanations for how and why they work. But doesn't this same reasoning also argue against the Christian belief in miracles? No, the Christian belief in miracles should not be equated with the New Age belief in pantheistic power for the following reasons:

    a. We do not believe in God as the cause of miraculous events for lack of scientific evidence, but because there is good reason to believe that the theistic God exists and that He is a miracle-making being.(See Norman L. Geisler, *Miracles and Modern Thought* (Grand Rapids: Zondervan, 1982); Norman L. Geisler and J. Kerby Anderson, *Origin Science: A Proposal for the Creation-Evolution Controversy* (Grand Rapids: Baker, 1987).

    b. While the mechanics of many providentially produced events can be naturalistically explained, the timing and purpose of the event makes it miraculous. Holistic health cannot boast the same kind of events.

19. Reisser, Reisser, and Weldon, *New Age Medicine,* 70-74.

20. Marcia Green, "Acupuncture," *SCP Newsletter* 10 (March-April 1984):9.

21. Thomas H. Makiyama, "Cut the Mumbo-Jumbo: What Is Ki?" *Black Belt,* May 1983, 79-80.

EIGHT
WHO WILL RULE THE EARTH?
The Dream of a Global Village

Dear Diary,

I fear that today may be my last entry. I was with a crowd of believers, and my son pointed me out to Lord Maitreya's police.

It seemed like such a good idea at first. Lord Maitreya promised love and peace. Our minds were afire with a kind of magical illumination. I myself experienced an out-of-body excursion.

He made us believe that we are all gods. No longer "god with us," he said, but "god in us." But I guess Lord Maitreya is the god of all gods. For now peace has turned to war, love to hate, and brotherhood into rape. I am still haunted by the memories of what he did—what we did—to those poor Christians.

Before Maitreya's men come, I must leave a warning behind. I recently discovered—there's a knock at the door.

NEW AGE GOAL OF A GLOBAL VILLAGE

New Agers leave no doubt that they are working for world unity. "We are the world," they sing as they attempt to overcome world hunger. After all, "This is the dawning of the Age of Aquarius," isn't it?

Just what would a New Age world look like? And how can we get there? The answer is that it would be one of new world cooperation brought about by a new world consciousness, a world of diversity in unity, one where each person realizes his own interdependence with the whole.

A New Spiritual Unity. According to New Age thought, there can be no world unity until each person discovers his own essential unity with every other person in the world community. "I am you, and you are me." When we each come to realize that at the depths of our beings we are all one, then world disharmony will cease. As Shirley MacLaine put it,

> *Maybe the tragedy of the human race was that we had forgotten we were each Divine. And if we realize that, we could dispel fear from our lives. In dispelling fear, we could dispel hate. And much more. With fear we would rid ourselves of greed and war and killing.* [1]

A New World Leader. Many New Agers look to a great world leader to help bring about the transition to the New Age. One such leader, Lord Maitreya, has been heralded as the New Age Christ. After July 19, 1977, full-page ads throughout the world read "THE CHRIST IS NOW HERE." Benjamin Creme declared that the New Age Christ will "save millions from death and misery through starvation," and will "release from bondage those now languishing in the prisons of the world for the 'crime' of independent thought." [2]

When this "Christ" appears he will "stimulate and inspire the formation of the New World Religion." [3] The world financial and economic order will be reconstructed when the New Age Messiah establishes the new order. [4]

A New Economic and Political Order. When this new christ-consciousness dawns on the world, it will lead to a new world order. The global manifestation of this spiritual unity will be a global cooperation among the governments of the world. Just as within a country the will of the individual is subordinated to that of the whole, this same principle will apply to countries within the world community.

Alice Bailey wrote,

> *In the coming world state, the individual citizen—gladly and deliberately and with full consciousness of all that he is doing— will subordinate his personality to the good of the whole.* [5]

World government is thus inevitable. However, such a global governing body will not be forced upon mankind. It will simply be the natural and logical extension of universal brotherhood. All the world will cooperate with each other to bring about the redistribution of world produce.[6]

CHRISTIAN REACTION TO THE GLOBAL VILLAGE CONCEPT

The temptation to see the New Age global goal as a fulfillment of biblical prophecy has been a temptation for many Christian writers. After all, the Bible seems to predict a one-world government and religion headed up by a dynamic world leader (Rev. 13; 17-18). He will sit in the temple of God claiming to be God (2 Thess. 2:4). So the New Age movement, in the estimation of such writers, must be the setup for the Antichrist.

Forecasts of Gloom and Doom. Many writers opposed to the New Age movement speak of "a very grim picture of the future."[7] The following are some somber, sad, and sinister examples of their forecasts:

> *We are referring to the "great delusion" that . . . will sweep the world in the "last days" and cause humanity to worship the Antichrist.[8]*

> *Our sole purpose is to expose a seduction that is gathering momentum and is no respecter of persons.[9]*

> *We are gravely concerned that millions of Christians are falling victim to the same delusion.[10]*

According to these prophets of gloom, "none of us is immune from being deceived and deceiving others."[11] The end of the world is at hand. The Antichrist is here. Watch out!

Identifying the Antichrist. Some anti-New Age writers identify the New Age movement with the coming of the biblically predicted Antichrist. According to Constance Cumbey,

> *For the first time in history there is a viable movement—the New Age movement—that truly meets all the scriptural requirements*

91

> *for the Antichrist and the political movement that will bring him
> on the world scene. It is further the position of the writer that this
> most likely is the great apostasy of "falling away" spoken of by
> the apostle Paul and that the Antichrist's appearance could be a
> real event in our immediate future.* [12]

Cumbey believes that Lord Maitreya is the Antichrist, claiming that Maitreya will proclaim himself as "Master Jesus" to the whole world.[13] This she believes will probably happen in the "immediate future.[14] Beyond this she is unwilling to go.

Other authors also yield to the temptation to identify the New Age movement with the religion of the Antichrist predicted in Scripture. Like Cumbey, Dave Hunt's "contrary scenario" identifies the New Age movement with the predicted "apostasy" found in 2 Thessalonians 2:3.[15] He goes so far as to say that "the Antichrist . . . is probably alive on planet earth today." Leading up to the end will be worldwide economic prosperity, ecological harmony, and peace.[16]

But this age of unprecedented prosperity will be a trap, a satanic counterfeit of the promised Millennium, a deceptive prelude to disaster. Just when all the earth is lulled into a false sense of security, "all hell will break loose!"[17]

Even the mighty U.S. of A. supposedly will collapse suddenly and mysteriously. No longer a major power, the American puppet nation, like all other nations, will bow down before a New Age Christ. Under the direction of a ruthless, vicious, totalitarian government, peace and love will turn into bloodshed and hate.[18]

For, according to Hunt, "the New Age Movement fits the description of the Antichrist's religion—a rejection of the Judeo-Christian God and the declaration that self is God."[19] Thus, the New Age movement's scientific mind technology is conditioning the world to accept the imminent satanic religion of the New Age Christ.[20]

PROPHESYING OR STUDYING PROPHECY?

One of the common assumptions of many anti-New Age prophets is the belief that we are in the "last days," or the period of the "church of Laodicea" at the end of the age just before Christ returns.[21] This belief, bolstered by the obvious fact that we are nearly two thousand years closer than the apostles were, gives them confidence in making these forecasts. However, there is a basic misunderstanding of Scripture involved here.

The Meaning of "Last Days." The phrase "last days" or "last hour" as used in the New Testament does not refer specifically to the end of the present age but to the whole age. It does not refer to the time just before Christ's second coming but to the whole time between His first and second comings. Consider the following passages in support of this contention:

First, Hebrews 1:1 says,

> God, who at various times and in different ways spoke in time past to the fathers by the prophets, has in these last days spoken to us by His Son, through whom also He made the world. (NKJV)

From this we can see that the phrase "last days" began during Christ's time on earth and will continue until He comes again. The former days are before Christ, and the later days are after He appeared. So, the "end time" had just as much scriptural support for occurring in the first century as it does today—no more, no less.

Second, in Acts 2 when Peter used Joel's prophecy about the "last days" he said to his hearers (in A.D. 33), "This is what was spoken of through the prophet Joel" (v. 16). But if Peter took this part of the prophecy about the "last days" to be fulfilled in the first century, then the last days must have begun then.

Third, in 1 John 2:18 the apostle warned his first-century readers, "Children, it is [now] the last hour." Then John alludes to the fact that there are many Antichrists in the world and adds, "From this we know that it is the last hour." But if the "last hour" included the first century, then it is obviously not limited to the twentieth century. If it was inclusive of the first part of this age, then it clearly is not limited to the last part of it.

Fourth, Paul told Timothy that he was living in the "later times," saying, "The Spirit explicitly says that in later times some will fall away from the faith, paying attention to deceiving spirits and doctrines of demons" (1 Tim. 4:1). Hence, if this moral and doctrinal decline was already present in Timothy's day, then it is wrong to speak of "last days" as though it refers particularly to our present day.

Confusing these predictions about the "last days" with our day generates a fatal error. It leads to the mistaken belief that when we see things happen that are predicted in the Bible, then we must be in the last days. This, of course, does not follow at all. For the phrase "last days" could include events that happened in any part of the time between Christ's first and second comings, including when He was on earth (Heb. 1:1), just after He ascended into heaven (Acts 2:16), just before He returns (2 Thess. 2), or even during His reign on earth (2 Pet. 3:10). But to assume that "last days" prophecies refer to the time just before Christ returns is to lay oneself open to the temptation to prophesy rather than to stick with studying prophecy.

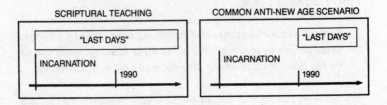

No One Knows the Day or the Hour. Jesus said clearly, "No one knows the day or hour" of His return, neither the angels nor the Son Himself (Matt. 24:36). How then do some anti-New Age writers conclude that we are living in the time "immediately prior" to Christ's return? The answer is that they misinterpret this passage and ignore another passage.

First, some add a qualifying word to what Jesus said, claiming that we are "unable to tell the exact 'day or hour' of His coming."[22] This, however, is adding to the Scriptures something that is not found in the text. But we must be very careful not to add to the Bible in order to justify our own views. Both the spirit and words of this passage oppose setting dates for Christ's return.

Second, most of those who are counting down to Armageddon ignore another passage in Scripture. They claim not to know the "day" on their calendar or the "hour" on their watch, but they do speak of the season or year of Christ's return. Besides violating the spirit of what Christ meant by the phrase "day and hour," this view flatly contradicts another declaration of Christ. One of the last things Jesus said to His disciples was that no one knows "the times [year] or seasons [of the year]." Nothing could be clearer: no one knows the day, hour, season, or year Christ will return. All four words for periods of time are used in these two texts to exclude the very thing many Christians are doing today—setting dates for the second coming of Christ.

Once when I was sharing this biblical truth with a well-known Christian author on popular end-times books, he gave the following startling response: "Jesus was just making an off-the-cuff statement here [in Acts 1:7] on which we should not base our belief about His return!" This is a shocking answer for one who claims to believe in the deity of Christ and the absolute authority of Scripture. But it reveals the extent to which one will go in justifying the unbiblical conclusion that we can count down the years before Armageddon. The truth of the matter is that Jesus is right: no one knows the time of His coming—not the Son, not the angels, and certainly not any Christian writers alive today.

LOOKING FOR CHRIST OR ANTICHRIST?

One of the problems with much of the anti-New Age material is that it engenders more consciousness of the Antichrist than of the Christ. Notice the number of references to the Antichrist in their writings. In one chapter we counted thirty-five occurrences of the word *Antichrist* (*Seduction,* chapter 4). Yet the word *Antichrist* occurs only four times in the entire Bible (1 John 2:18, 22; 4:3; 2 John 7)!

Hope vs. Fear. Contrary to the Scriptures that were written that we might have hope (Rom. 15:4), this unhealthy focus on the sinister end-time figure leaves the reader with more fear than hope.

Take the following pronouncement as an example: "Satan or demons . . . will hide behind any mask and answer to any image or name."[23] Another anti-New Ager, Texe Marrs, claims that "the New Age ideology lends itself to extremes, causing a person to first wax sweet, then vengeful when demons stir up the aggressive traits latent in every man who does not have Christ within."[24] This kind of fear-engendering remark is spooky at best and kooky at worst. We must be careful not to look for a demon on every doorknob or a spook of apostasy in every closet. This creates unnecessary suspicion in believers, from whose hearts God's love "casts out fear, because fear involves torment" (1 John 4:18, NKJV).

When studying prophecy we should come away with more hope in Christ than fear of the Antichrist. We should not have anxiety but expectation. For "hope does not disappoint, because the love of God has been poured out within our hearts through the Holy Spirit who was given to us" (Rom. 5:5).

The Uppertaker, Not the Undertaker. The New Testament Christian was not looking for the Antichrist but was waiting for Christ. Paul exhorted Titus to keep "looking for the blessed hope and glorious appearing of our great God and Savior Jesus Christ" (Titus 2:13, NKJV). The young

Thessalonian Christians were told by God "to wait for His Son from heaven . . . that is Jesus, who delivers us from the wrath to come" (1 Thess. 1:10). Likewise, John encouraged the believers saying, "We know when He is revealed, we shall be like Him, for we shall see Him as He is. And everyone who has this hope in Him purifies himself, just as He is pure" (1 John 3:2-3, NKJV).

The focus of the New Testament is not on the coming woes to be inflicted on the world by the Antichrist but on the coming wonders to be given to believers by the Christ. We are not looking for the undertaker but the "Uppertaker," the One who will catch us away to heaven (1 Thess. 4:13-17) and deliver us from the wrath to come (1 Thess. 5:9).

Gloom or Glory? Consider this somber statement:

> *Christianity may well be facing the greatest challenge in its history: a series of powerful and growing seductions that are subtly changing biblical interpretations and undermining the faith of millions of people.* "[25]

This kind of sensationalized sadism is not spiritually edifying to the saints. In fact, it is more discouraging to the disciples of Christ. Realizing the somber tone, one anti-New Age writer confessed, "as 'negative' as it sounds, Antichrist will rule the earth."[26] True as this is, it is misleading when not placed in context. Antichrist will only rule for a few short years; Christ will reign for a "for ever and ever" (Rev. 11:15). Hence, to stress the infinitesimally short reign of evil over against the eternal dominion of good is lopsided and unhealthy.

Long-range Optimism and Short-range Pessimism. It is true that the Bible predicts a great time of war and tribulation is coming upon the earth (Matt. 24:21). But it also says it will be followed by eternal tranquility (Rev. 21-22). Sure, things will get worse before they get better (2 Tim. 3:13). But when they get better, they are going to be really good! And with a short exception at the end of the Millennium (Rev. 20:7-10) they are going to stay good forever (Rev. 20-22). So why be short-range pessimists when we should be long-range optimists? Sure, the great Tribulation is coming, but so is the Millennium right on its tail. Certainly in this world we shall have tribulation (John 15:18f.). But we must remember the words of Paul: "Our light affliction, which is but for a moment, is working for us a far more exceeding and eternal weight of glory" (2 Cor. 4:17, NKJV). It is glory, not gloom, that the Bible holds out for the believers. Hence, it is not the trials of time but the ecstasy of eternity that should be stressed for believers.

Many of the current prophets of gloom and doom are reminiscent of the people who can only see one small dot and not the whole white page around it. New Agers will not be in charge of the global village, for God is in charge of the New Age. History is His story. God is in sovereign control of human history and destiny (Dan. 2; 7). His purposes cannot be thwarted. Job confessed to God: "I know that you can do everything, and that no purposes of Yours can be withheld from You" (Job 42:2, NKJV). The psalmist added, "Whatever the Lord pleases, He does, in heaven and in earth, in the seas and in all deeps" (Ps. 135:6).

Cursing Darkness or Lighting Candles? When all is said and done about the New Age movement, there is more said than done. Furthermore, there is more said negatively than there is done positively. More time is spent cursing New Age darkness than lighting Christian candles. Jesus said to His disciples, "You are the light of the world" (Matt. 5:14). Darkness cannot extinguish light. On the contrary, darkness flees with the least little flicker of light.

In writings on the New Age there is too much warning about unbelief in God and not enough encouraging of belief in God. In stark contrast the Scriptures speak of the future in expectant terms, saying: "We who are alive and remain shall be caught up together with them [believers already dead] in the clouds to meet the Lord in the air, and thus we shall always be with the Lord" (1 Thess. 4:17).

Words That Comfort, Not Clobber. When speaking about the future the apostle held out comfort not despair. He said, "Comfort one another with these words." In the very book so often quoted about the coming apostasy, Paul spoke of "hope in our Lord Jesus Christ" (1 Thess. 1:3). Indeed, he triumphantly declares, "What is our hope, or joy, or crown of rejoicing? Is it not even you in the presence of our Lord Jesus Christ at His coming" (1 Thess. 2:19). These are words that comfort, not clobber. They build up, not tear down.

James Patterson has nicely summed up the problems with conspiracy theories:

In the final analysis, apocalyptic conspiracy theories poorly serve both history and prophecy. Historians prefer complex and multidimensional explanations of the past, whereas conspiracy models are inherently simplistic. In addition, conspiracy approaches are historically conditioned and thus tend to lose their plausibility with the passage of time. The conspiratorial motifs of American Protestantism, where testable through historical hindsight, have been proven wrong. History simply does not conform to the neat and tidy specifications of conspiracy theories.

Conspiratorial models also trivialize the richness of biblical prophecy. Where the apocalyptic texts of Scripture utilize symbols and even veiled language, the advocates of conspiracy theories attempt detailed and highly speculative applications of such texts to current events. In the process the prophetic message of the Bible loses some of its sting and can even become captive to political and national agendas. Ultimately, as the Scriptures affirm, there is a cosmic conspiracy against the kingdom of God. But this conspiracy is far more subtle, far more extensive, and not so easily identifiable as the apocalypticists would have us believe.[27]

Much of the current thinking about seduction seems itself to be seduced into warning Christians but failing to properly encourage them. But the Bible was written "that through perseverance and the encouragement of the Scriptures we might have hope" (Rom. 15:4). Thus the Bible does not concentrate on the seduction by the Enemy (Satan) but on salvation by our Friend (Christ) who loved us and gave himself for us (Titus 2:14). For "greater love has no one than this, than one lay down his life for his friends" (John 15:13).

Christ's Triumph and Satan's Defeat. The Christian message is one of victory, not defeat. Christ has already defeated Satan and all his hosts at the Cross. Their power is not only limited and hedged by a sovereign God (Job 1:10) but they are doomed (Rev. 19-20). Christ "led captivity captive" (Eph. 4:8, KJV) and "disarmed" demons (Col. 2:15). They know their ultimate doom (Matt. 8:29). And Satan is aware "he has only a short time" (Rev. 12:12). By His death and powerful resurrection Christ has destroyed death and robbed its power from Satan (Heb. 2:14). He has "brought life and immortality to light through the gospel" (2 Tim. 1:10).

If then the hordes of hell are aware of their defeat by Christ and of their inevitable doom and damnation in the lake of fire (Rev. 19:20), then why are Christians so fearful of Satan's deluding activity? We have nothing to fear except this kind of fear itself. Indeed, John said, "Perfect love casts out fear" (1 John 4:18). But the current seduction literature is unwittingly encouraging fear of the future and fear of the Devil. In this sense Dave Hunt's warning that "none of us is immune from being deceived and deceiving others" must be taken seriously.[28] Is it possible that those warning about the seduction of Satan could be seduced themselves? Is it possible that they have exposed the Enemy (Satan) in such a way as to be seduced by the Enemy? One thing is certain: Undue attention on Antichrist can cause us to lose our proper focus on Christ. We must never become so Satan conscious that we lose our consciousness of Christ. If we do, this would be one of the more clever tricks of the Master Deceiver (Gen. 3).

IS THERE A WORLD CONSPIRACY?

It seems obvious that Christians spend far too much time on tracking down conspiracies and instigating witch hunts. Is there a communist conspiracy? Are the secular humanists plotting to take over America? Is there a New Age conspiracy? Who is behind it all?

The Prince of the Power of the Air. As far as the Bible is concerned there is only one real conspiracy—a spiritual one. Satan has conspired against God. He and his angels have been thrown out of heaven (Rev. 12:7-9), and they have gone out to deceive the world (1 Pet. 5:8). So there is a worldwide conspiracy, but it is neither communist nor humanist. It is neither capitalist nor New Age. It is a spiritual conspiracy. Satan backs anything that attacks God. He is for anything that is against Christ. As the apostle Paul put it, "For our struggle is not against flesh and blood, but against the rulers, against the powers, against the world forces of this darkness, against the spiritual forces of wickedness in the heavenly places" (Eph. 6:12).

Of course, Satan does not work in a vacuum. He works through the evil world system that appeals to our sinful selves. There is much wisdom in Os Guinness's comment about our real enemy:

> *Our real enemy today is not secularism, not humanism, not Marxism, not any of the great religious rivals to the Christian gospel, not even modernization, but ourselves. We who are Western Christians are simply a special case of a universal human condition to*

*which Pascal [the French Christian philosopher] pointed earlier.
"Jesus Christ comes to tell men that they have no enemies but themselves." Or as it has been put more recently: "We have met the enemy
and it is us."*[29]

The Fallacy of Conspiracy Theories. As for political conspiracy theories,
the Christian would be well advised to avoid an unhealthy interest in them
for several reasons. First, it is an unproductive sidetrack for the Christian life. Souls are perishing and Christ is coming. We do not have time
to trace endless charts and seek to find relationships between earthly political powers. It can unnecessarily consume our precious time (Col. 4:5).
And it is a fruitless effort in view of Christ's victory over all powers and
dominions and thrones (Eph. 1:21). It is sufficient for us to know that
the Devil and his hosts are defeated and that we can overcome by the
spiritual armor of God (Eph. 6:14-15).

Second, there are opposing groups, all of which are allegedly in secret control of the world. Once it was the Nazis and then the communists.
Now we have the Illuminati and the Club of Rome. We also have both
secular humanists and New Agers. But they cannot all be the secret
power, for they have opposing beliefs. Secular humanists are opposed
to communists' suppression of freedom. Since New Agers are pantheists,
they oppose both secular humanists and communists, who are atheistic
or agnostic. So even the so-called conspirators are not in agreement.

CONCLUSION

Much Christian energy is unnecessarily spent on political conspiracy
theories, looking for invisible governments, and trying to identify the
coming Antichrist. This is unbiblical, unfruitful, and unnecessary. It
is unbiblical because no one knows the time of Christ's return, not even
Christ Himself (Matt. 24:36). It is unfruitful because it is a tangent to
our real task. It so easily sidetracks Christians from the real spiritual
warfare. And often it generates more awareness of Satan than of Christ.
Finally, it is unnecessary, since Satan is a defeated foe. "Greater is He
who is in you than he who is in the world" (1 John 4:4). The Christian
fixation should not be the coming Antichrist, but the coming of Christ,
who "will soon crush Satan under your feet" (Rom. 16:20).

Notes

1. Shirley MacLaine, *Out on a Limb* (New York: Bantam, 1983), 347.
2. Benjamin Creme, *The Reappearance of the Christ and the Masters of Wisdom* (North Hollywood, Calif.: Tara Center, 1980), 37.
3. Ibid., 169.
4. Ibid., 34.
5. Alice Bailey, *Education in the New Age* (New York: Lucis, 1954), 122.
6. Creme, *Reappearance,* 169.
7. Dave Hunt and T. A. McMahon, *The Seduction of Christianity* (Eugene, Oreg.: Harvest House, 1985), 63.
8. Ibid., 7.
9. Ibid.
10. Ibid., 9.
11. Ibid., 213.
12. Constance Cumbey, *The Hidden Dangers of the Rainbow* (Shreveport, La.: Huntington House, 1983), 7.
13. Ibid., 22.
14. Ibid., 39.
15. Dave Hunt, *Peace, Prosperity, and the Coming Holocaust* (Eugene, Oreg.: Harvest House, 1983), 72.
16. Ibid., 36.
17. Ibid., 36-37.
18. Ibid., 47.
19. Ibid., 72.
20. Hunt and McMahon, *Seduction of Christianity,* 53.
21. Ibid., 221.
22. Ibid., 36.
23. Ibid., 167.
24. Texe Marrs, *Dark Secrets of the New Age* (Westchester, Ill.: Crossway, 1987), 155.
25. Hunt and McMahon, *Seduction,* 11.
26. Ibid., 48.
27. James Alan Patterson, "Changing Images of the Beast: Apocalyptic Conspiracy Theories in American History," *JETS,* December 1988: 443.
28. Ibid., 213.
29. Os Guinness, *The Gravedigger File: Papers on the Subversion of the Modern Church* (Downers Grove, Ill.: InterVarsity, 1983), 1

EPILOGUE
NEW EARTH
*A Christian Vision of the Renewed World,
Based on Revelation 21–22*

Date: A.D.R.[1] 1892

Nearly two millenniums have passed since Armageddon. Peace has reigned, and eternal bliss is no longer a utopian dream. It has been a reality for these many years. That which was written long ago has come to pass: "And He shall wipe away every tear from their eyes; and there shall no longer be any death; there shall no longer be any mourning, or crying, or pain; the first things have passed away."

My staff and I are keepers of the history of humankind. Since the return of our Lord and beginning of his millennial reign, I have overseen the holy records. I have witnessed the final fall of the Evil One at the end of the millennial kingdom and celebrated the second genesis.

In many ways, it is odd to think that records are needed in New Earth. Everything is perfect here. There literally is no sin in the world. Humans of New Earth are living out the rewarding consequences of their decisions to trust in Lord Jesus for their redemption. Though I witnessed the chain of events myself, I have yet to fathom it. Yes, records are needed even now, but for different reasons than Old Earth. Israel needed reminders of Yahweh's faithfulness. Christians needed reminders of the Lord's future promises. Old Earth needed records to help them in their war with sin. But in the new world, where all are perfect, records are used for richer understanding and greater appreciation. And so I watch. And I write.

Infinite joy is part of being perfect created beings. New creations, yes, but creatures nonetheless. We are like Him without being Him. Our transformation still astounds me! New bodies, renewed minds, yet our individuality, personality, talents, and gifts still intact. Only the original Architect could redesign His work without destroying its essence.

Our once frail vessels are now strong. Our minds now behold the face of God. Our cup is full with the infinite joy of God. And though no creature could ever be equal to God in power, wisdom, love, and splendor, we are as close as creatures can be. And that is far more than anyone could experience and enjoy even for an eternity.

On New Earth all humans love each other without compromising truth, they commune with God without losing their identities, they realize that God is not found in their mirrors, but in the miracles of His revelation. And His revelation is clearer to humans than ever before. It's not that He speaks louder or more often, so much as humans are now able to withstand His brilliant light and thundering voice. Illumination is now a human condition. Humans can see God and live.

In New Earth, artists passionately communicate the beauty and wonder of the new world. Business and government carry on without self-interest and corruption. Recreation reaches new depths of excitement and adventure. New Earth has not negated the human activity of Old Earth, but only those elements that were good and right and noble survived the transformation of new genesis. All the pain, toil, and ugliness were burnt up along with the disease, deterioration, and degeneration of Old Earth. There is no end to the pleasures of God.

New Earth itself is an endless breathtaking wonder. All the beauty of Old Earth without the tragedy. Majestic mountains to climb, lush fields, and while oceans no longer exist, there are plenty of lakes and ponds.

Even the Holy City, Jerusalem, has been made new. Twelve of us keep watch over the gates of a great wall that stands over two hundred feet high. The crystal-clear jasper wall reflects the rainbow of colors from the foundation stones of jasper, sapphire, chalcedony, emerald, sardonyx, sardius, chrysolite, beryl, topaz, chrysoprase, jacinth, and amethyst. Capping the north, south, west, and east entrances are twelve gates, each made from a single pearl.

The city itself is 1,500 square miles of pure gold. The gold of the city and its street is so pure that it shines like clear glass. In the middle of the street stands the Tree of Life, preserved through all the ages to take its place in restored Paradise. The Tree of Life flanks the river of the water of life, which flows from the throne of God and Jesus Christ.

The temple no longer exists because God is the temple. God is present among His people, and His delight is upon this place. I find it difficult to remember much of the old world, except as a faint reflection of the new. The brilliance and beauty of New Earth overpowers the memory of Old Earth as a kiss dispels one's tears. When evil was judged and put away forever, God worked a miracle that will never be duplicated again. We heard Him say, "Behold, I am making all things new."

At once the restoration of creation commenced. New Earth burst forth from its dying womb. A new age had begun. A new age where all present confess Jesus Christ as Lord. All alien elements were dispelled from its glorious presence. A world where hate, ignorance, and rebellion are long forgotten relics of the first genesis. Night disappeared into the pages of human history never to envelop the light of day again. Even the sun could not withstand the transformation of the new creation because it was far too cold and dim compared to the glory of its Creator. Thus was born . . . the dawning of the new heaven and new earth.

Notes

1. A.D.R.=Anno Domini Reditus—in the year of the Lord's return.

√ Steve agrees

√ Steve disagrees

√ Requires further study

√ Irrelevant → not a valid
New Age Belief

APPENDIX ONE
A SUMMARY OF NEW
AGE BELIEFS

This section can be used as a reference to basic New Age beliefs. For the sake of clarity and space limitations, we have only presented representative quotes. More detailed explanations and evaluations of these beliefs are given in the main text of this book.

New Age spokesmen are not a unified front, and no statement quoted here is necessarily the belief of every person involved in the New Age movement. As pointed out below, God is often conceived of as an impersonal force, yet other writers speak of a personal God. Many New Age devotees delight in such inconsistencies. In fact, part of the New Age appeal is the freedom from logic and any kind of orthodox thinking. This is inevitable, since the traditional Western concern for reason and logic is abandoned for the Eastern way, which is comfortable with contradictions and inconsistencies. Still, the quotes here can be said to represent typical New Age thought.

KNOWLEDGE OF THE TRUTH

We must not be hindered by the strictures of logical thinking.

> *It was becoming more and more clear to me that to call one point of view the only true reality was limited, prejudiced, and probably incorrect.* [1]

You must learn to trust your feelings more and refrain from approaching so many issues in life from strictly an intellectual perspective. Intellect as a marvel is limited. . . . Feelings are limitless. Trust your heart . . . or your intuition, as you term it.[2]

If people insist upon remaining within their "logical" belief systems they are safe within their own perceived reality, and thus are safe within the position of power they hold, whatever that power might be. They will not change their perceptions and thus be required to change themselves or grow into an expanded awareness of themselves.[3]

I began to feel (rather than to think about) a new way of looking at life and myself.[4]

The mind, with all its potential ramifications, was the great limiter. . . . Too much thinking was simply a handicap.[5]

I was aware at all times that everyone else was pursuing their own path, consciously or unconsciously. They had their own perceptions, their own truth, their own pace, and their own version of enlightenment. It was not possible to judge another's truth.[6]

Stop judging and evaluating what you're getting at. Leave your mind out of this. Just get out of your intellectual way.[7]

REVELATION

The Bible is incomplete and inadequate.

Little as the orthodox Christian may care to admit it, the entire Gospel story in its four forms or presentations, contains little else except symbolic details about the Mysteries.[8]

Special revelation continues today through many New Age prophets.

Visel the holy one who commissioned Levi: "Behold the Akasha! Behold the Record Galleries of Visel where every thought and word and deed of every living thing is written down. . . . Now, Levi, hearken to my words: go forth into these mystic Galleries and read. There you will find a message for the world; for every man; for every living thing. I breathe upon you now the Holy Breath; you will discriminate, and you will know the lessons that these Record Books of God are keeping now for men of this new age. . . . Now, Levi, message bearer of the Spirit Age, take up our pen and write."[9]

And when the world is ready to receive, lo, God will send a messenger to open up the book and copy from its sacred pages all the messages of Purity and Love. Then every man of earth will read the words of life in the language of his native land, and men will see the light.[10]

Akasha is a Sanskrit word, and means "Primary Substance," that out of which all things are formed. . . . The imperishable records of life, known as the Akashic Records, are wholly in the domain of Supreme Intelligence, or Universal Mind, and the Akashic Record reader must be in such close touch with the Holy Spirit, or the Holy Breath, as the ancient masters call this spirit of Supreme Intelligence, that every thought vibration is instantly felt in every fiber of his being.[11]

It descends on me and comes down as far as the solar plexus and a kind of cone is formed, like that, in light. There is an emotional outflow as well. It is the mental overshadowing which produces the rapport so that I can hear, inwardly, the words. The astral overshadowing allows what is called the True Spirit of the Christ, the energy of the Cosmic Christ, to flow out to the audience to the world. . . . I am aware of His Presence, I can sense part of His mind in my mind. It is difficult to describe, but it is there.[12]

I would like to say in preface that I am not a channel or a medium. It is not through any kind of trance that I receive that which I receive when it comes in this form. It is through a process of my own meditation in which I experience something and then it is up to me to put the experience into words and to put it in as best a context of verbalization as I can manage. Therefore, the words that I am going to quote are words inspired in my consciousness by the experience I was having, but are not to be considered actual direct quotes from the divine. That which the divine says is essen-

tially wordless and each of us cloak it in whatever form is most appropriate. [13]

In my own case, the ability to commune between dimensions developed naturally out of a childhood sensitivity and led me as a teenager into exploring the esoteric and mystical traditions more consciously. This in turn resulted in my becoming a lecturer on esoteric themes, with particular reference to the dawning of a New Age in our time, the emergence of a new cycle of human consciousness and experience for which our troubled century was a period of transformation and transition. [14]

It was at such a meeting on the 31st of July, 1970, that I became aware on the fringes of my consciousness of a strong presence that was overlighting the proceedings. I shared what I was feeling, and we decided to sit in meditation together and see if this presence could be contacted . . . the result was communion with an impersonal consciousness that identified itself through the qualities of Limitless Love and Truth. Within that communion, I was able to identify and to communicate the ideas and vision which this presence embodied.

    This contact continued off and on through September 3rd, 1970, resulting in seven transmissions in all. . . . The other six transmissions all deal with the transition into a New Age, the birth of a new world and a new consciousness, the descent of higher energies of spirit into human consciousness and so forth. [15]

When I sat down to write, I envisioned a publication of about twenty to thirty pages. I had no intention of writing a book. However, as I began, it was as if I were overlighted by another aspect of this presence of Limitless Love and Truth. Insights which I had gained over the years through my communions with higher levels, new information, and a deeper identification with some of the processes behind that presence all came together in a synthesis of inspiration, and I found myself writing non-stop for several days. [16]

In all honesty I was embarrassed by this. In the first place, I had tried hard all my life to deglamorize my contact with other levels, to avoid being thought of as a "channel" or a psychic medium. Just as that contact was very normal for me, I felt it important to convey that normalcy and help others find similar attunement within themselves. To be thought of as a prophet or a seer seemed to work against that intention. [17]

I found that my consciousness came into contact with a force or a presence. It could not be accurately described as being but definitely as a point of revelation, a mirror of sorts. This resulted in six statements of vision, six communications, which were put out in little booklets from Findhorn and which inspired a number of questions. In an attempt to answer the questions I ended up writing the book called, Revelation: The Birth of a New Age. [18]

Never has Deity left Itself at any time without witness. Never has man demanded light that the light has not been forthcoming. Never has there been a time, cycle or world period when there was not the giving out of the teaching and spiritual help which human need demanded. [19]

It required many years for Levi to learn the Law of Differentiation, and to come in rapport with the tones and rhythms of Jesus of Nazareth, Enoch and Melchizedek and their co-laborers. But under the direction of the Spirit of Supreme Intelligence, he has attained unto this accomplishment, and now he instantly feels in all his being the slightest vibrations that come from any of these great centers and, of course, all of his transcriptions are true to the letter. [20]

New Age revelation is superior to Scripture.

No other revelation to equal it has been offered to humanity, but all revelations of the past have led up to it. Jesus gave the great bridge through proclaiming our kinship with God, our sonship with him. Buddha gave the great bridge in enabling us to find the balance of our own being so that the energies we receive are expressed in harmony with the whole. Through knowing wisdom and through knowing love we now should be at the point, and we are at the point, where God can reasonably say to us, "All right, I have given you the keys. I have given you the tools. Now build with me." [21]

The New Age is essentially a time in planetary history when the fruits of revelation given and anchored by Jesus come into being. In human terms, this means it is a time when we learn to be at one with God ourselves, to be Christs ourselves. This is also the revelation of esoteric disciplines, which have always been esoteric because they dealt with the reality of man's inner divinity and how to actualize it, rather than with the forms and doctrines relating to forming relationships with an external deity or Christ. Yet orthodox Christianity has a strong mystical side that, to the best of its ability, has taught the imitation of Christ. It has not fully dared the cosmic breadth of Jesus' revelation ("Ye are gods." "All that I do, you shall do, and greater.") [and] has suggested imitation of Jesus, not actually being the Christ.[22]

GOD

God is everything and everything is God.

God is the sum total of all that exists in the whole of the manifested and unmanifested universe — everything we know and see and hear and touch and everything we don't know or hear or see or touch, everywhere, in the totality of the cosmos. Every manifested phenomenon is part of God. And the space between these manifested phenomena is God. So, in a very real sense, there isn't anything else. You are God. I am God. This microphone is God. This table is God. All is God. And because all is God, there is no God. God is not someone that you can point to and say "That is God." God is everything that you have ever known or could ever know — and everything beyond your level of knowing.[23]

Am I God? Am I a Christ? Am I a Being come to you from the dwelling places of the Infinite? I am all these things, yet more.[24]

One of the major teachings of the Christ [is] the fact of God immanent, immanent in all creation, in mankind and all creation, that there is nothing else but God; that we are all part of a great Being.[25]

God, or the God Force, of which all things are a part . . . is the Divine Energy that created the Universe and holds it together harmoniously.[26]

This Source fills and organizes all life. It is the beginning and the end; the Alpha and the Omega. It is the God of Creation. And it is very much in us.[27]

What is Limitless Love? Surely it is that presence which has been before the foundations of the earth and shall remain after this planet has entered yet another cycle in the far distant future of your time. I am timeless and infinite. There is no place that knows me not. There is no time when I have not expressed what I am. I am the root of you, I am the stem of you, the flowering and the seed that goes forth. I am all that you are. You will receive my energy and it shall dwell within you and make you one.[28]

God is energy, as everything is energy.

"God is energy" is equally a fact. Love—what we call love—is a great energy, a great magnetic all-pervading energy.[29]

Some New Agers describe God as eternal, impersonal, infinite, and unchanging (pantheism).

The Secret Doctrine *establishes three fundamental postulates. The first is the existence of an omnipresent, eternal, boundless and immutable Principle on which all speculation is impossible, since it transcends the power of human conception and can only be dwarfed by any human expression or similitude. It is beyond the range of thought, unspeakable and unthinkable.[30]*

Other times, God is described as a changing God, ever growing and increasing. This means that God is actually finite though potentially infinite (panentheism).

I want to grow out of a man to be a god, to lose my manhood, to merge into godhood; and when I become a god, I shall still have,

I hope, this yearning, this unsatisfied hunger for something grander and greater still than godhood, always marching upwards and onwards. [31]

[God] is revelation and revelation is an ongoing, ever-revealing, dynamic process. Revelation is the mirror that shows us what we are so that through that understanding we can continually unfold and reveal the divine. That is the best definition of God: that which is dynamically unfolding and revealing the wholeness that is. [32]

Interdependent relationship between God and humankind: God needs man just as man needs God. (Note that in this context God is personal, even though, as noted above, God is often portrayed as impersonal.)

A fourth essential truth and one which clarifies all the planned work of the Christ is tied in with spiritual revelation and the need of man for God and of God for man. [33]

The Law of Love, according to the Hierarchy, is the basic law governing our existence. We live in a solar system Whose nature is Love. The Christ came 2,000 years ago to show a new aspect of God, that aspect we call Love. He showed God as a loving father—not an old man with a beard, of course—Whose nature is essentially Love. Love is an energy, a great cosmic energy which streams from the Heart of the Sun. [34]

Many New Agers speak of a source beyond God that is impersonal and all-pervading.

It is not Being; it is not a personality; it is not the Christ. It is not God. It incorporates and is blended with the essence of many Beings and ultimately of all Beings. It is of the Christ and an expression of Divinity. In its communication with you this day through the focus of your consciousnesses, it partakes of the energies of your higher selves . . . your minds and hearts, and of the energies of others who, though not physically present, attune to your focus. It draws on the planetary network of world servers which exists on the inner and which is in the process of externalization onto the outer planes. It draws on myself and on others greater than I. In short, this presence is a number of things as it seeks sufficient personification to address you; perhaps it could be called not only Limitless Love and Truth but the presence of the indwelling self of humanity, seeking to address its energies in a particular way at this time through an image of a New Age which represents another stage in the process of that self's unfoldment through history. Thus, we could call this presence the spirit or image of the New Age. [35]

The New Age Trinity is not the traditional Christian Trinity.

The Spirit of eternity is One unmanifest; and this is God the Father, God the Mother, God the Son in One. In life of manifests the One became the Three, and God the Father is the God of might; and God the Mother is omniscient God, and God the Son is love. And God the Father is the power of heaven and earth; and God the Mother is the Holy Breath, the thought of heaven and earth; and God the Son, the only son, is Christ, and Christ is love. [36]

CHRIST

Christ is virtually eliminated from the redemption scheme for all humankind. New Agers reject the biblical teaching that Christ sacrificed his life in order to bring us forgiveness of sins. In fact, Jesus of Nazareth and Christ are two separate entities. The man Jesus is separate and distinct from the Christ Spirit.

[The Christ spirit dwelt in] Hercules, Hermes, Rama, Mitra . . . Krishna, Buddha, and the Christ. [All these were] perfect men in their time, all sons of men who become Sons of God, for having revealed their innate Divinity. [37]

The historical Christ, then, is a glorious Being belonging to the great spiritual hierarchy that guides the spiritual evolution of humanity, who used for some three years the human body of the disciple Jesus . . . who was finally put to death for blasphemy, for teaching the inherent Divinity of Himself and of all men. [38]

In the esoteric tradition the Christ is not the name of an individual but of an office in the Hierarchy.[39]

There is a growing and developing belief that Christ is in us, as He was in the Master Jesus, and this belief will alter world affairs and mankind's entire attitude to life.[40]

Jesus is not unique

All men are innate divinity . . . so that in time all men become christs.[41]

Jesus is divine in exactly the sense that we are divine.[42]

Christ was the most advanced human ever to walk on this planet.[43]

Christ said, "I am your Friend and Brother, not a God."[44]

It is claimed that when a woman knelt to worship Jesus, he replied, "Good woman, stay; take heed to what you do; you may not worship man; this is idolatry."[45]

[Christ supposedly said,] "What I have done, all men will do; and what I am, all men will be."[46]

The Christ is not God. When I say, "the coming of Christ," I don't mean the coming of God, I mean the coming of a divine man, a man who has manifested His divinity by the same process that we are going through—the incarnational process, gradually perfecting Himself.[47]

Christ is the same force as Lucifer.

Christ is the same force as Lucifer but moving in seemingly the opposite direction. Lucifer moves in to create the light within through the pressure of experience. Christ moves out to release that light, that wisdom, that love into creation so what has been forged in the furnace of creation can become a light unto the world and not simply stagnate within being.[48]

Jesus did not die and therefore did not physically resurrect.

Write of his [Jesus'] works as prophet, priest and seer; write of his life of purity and love, and how he changed his carnal flesh to flesh divine without descending through the gates of death.[49]

He [Jesus] was despised, rejected and abused; was spit upon, was crucified, was buried in a tomb; but he revived and rose a conqueror over death that he might show the possibilities of man.[50]

HUMAN NATURE

Humans are basically spiritual rather than material beings. We are energy.

The spiritual being, Man, descended from a subtler plane to assume a body, the necessary sheath in which to live amid earth vibrations.[51]

[The body is] a manifest; is the result of force; it is but naught; is an illusion, nothing more.[52]

This energy [the Divine Force] is the energy that makes up the soul. Our bodies are made out of atoms; our souls are made of this Source energy.[53]

The body died . . . the soul's energy lived eternally. So, that must mean we are our souls—the body only houses the soul.[54]

There is an ancient occult axiom which says that there is nothing in the whole of the manifested universe but energy, in some relationship or other, some frequency or other.[55]

We are divine; we are christs.

Slowly, there is dawning upon the awakening consciousness of humanity, the great paralleling truth of God Immanent—divinely "pervading" all forms, conditioning from within all kingdoms in nature, expressing innate divinity through human beings and—two thousand years ago—portraying the nature of that divine Immanence in the Person of the Christ. Today, as an outcome of this unfolding divine Presence, there is entering into the minds of men everywhere a new concept: that of Christ in us, the hope of Glory. There is a growing and developing belief that Christ is in us, as He was in the Master Jesus, and this belief will alter world affairs and mankind's entire attitude to life.[56]

All men are innate divinity . . . so that in time all men become christs.[57]

Man is a thought of God; all thoughts of God are infinite; they are not measured by time; for things that are concerned with time begin and end.[58]

A thousand times he [Jesus] said to men: "I came to show the possibilities of man; what I have done all men may do, and what I am all men shall be."[59]

At the Transfiguration Christ revealed the glory which is innate in all men.[60]

Jesus said, "What I can do all men can do. Go preach the gospel of the omnipotence of Man."[61]

One doesn't pray to oneself, one prays to the God within. The thing is to learn to invoke that energy which is the energy of God. Prayer and worship as we know it today will gradually die out and men will be trained to invoke the power of Deity. This is one reason why the Great Invocation was given out — to enable us to learn the technique of invocation.[62]

Within the inner heart one finds God, peace, and oneself. . . . The self, however, knows the Divine truth because the self is itself Divine.[63]

You are God. You know you are Divine. But you must continually remember your Divinity and, most important, act accordingly.[64]

The higher unlimited superconsciousness can best be defined as one's eternal unlimited soul — the soul that is the real "you." The soul that has been through incarnation after incarnation and knows

*all there is to know about you because it is you. It is the repository
of your experience. It is the totality of your soul memory and your
soul energy. It is also the energy that interfaces with the energy
which we refer to as God. It knows and resonates to God because
it is a part of God. As in the mind of man there are many thoughts,
so in the mind of God there are many souls.*[65]

We need to trust the fact that we are "indeed unlimited."[66]

*It's all inside of you. Just listen to your feelings and trust them.
You are unlimited. You just don't realize it.*[67]

*We are not under the law of God. We are as the law of God. We
are God.*[68]

*Recognizing the God within myself, I will recognize the larger God-
source, the magnificent energy which unites us all.*[69]

*I am God, because all energy is plugged in to the same source.
We are each aspects of that source. We are all part of God. We are
all individualized reflections of the God source. God is us and we
are God.*[70]

*Each soul is its own God. You must never worship anyone or any-
thing other than self. For you are God. To love self is to love
God.*[71]

SIN AND MORALITY

**Moral values are relative and are dependent on the will of man, not
the nature of God.**

In a spiritual state, morality is impossible.[72]

*[New Age ethics] is not based on . . . dualistic concepts of "good"
or "bad."*[73]

*Until mankind realizes there is, in truth, no good and there is, in
truth, no evil—there will be no peace.*[74]

There really is no such thing as sin (breaking of moral law) and evil.

> *Man holds the ultimate responsibility for the redemption of what we have come to call "evil energies," which are simply energies that have been used out of timing or out of place, or not suited to the needs of evolution.* [75]

> *Evil is only the inharmonious blending of the colors, tones, or forms of good.* [76]

> *There is no such thing as evil. Evil is fear and uncertainty. Evil is what you think it is.* [77]

> *What you are calling evil is really only the lack of consciousness of God. The question is lack of spiritual knowledge, not whether or not there is evil.* [78]

> *Evil is nothing but energy flowing backward rather than forward. Spell your live backward and you have evil.* [79]

Our present problems are rooted in "evil" deeds performed in past reincarnations. This is called "karma."

> *[Karmic justice] would have explained all the suffering and horror in the world which all my life had rendered me helplessly incapable of understanding or altering.* [80]

> *The purpose of getting in touch with past-life experience, then, is to isolate the areas of emotional discord so that the conflict in relation to today's incarnation can be understood.* [81]

Our ultimate problem is that we forgot our divinity.

> *The tragedy of the human race . . . was that we had forgotten we were each Divine.* [82]

> *Everything in life is the result of either illumination or ignorance. Those are the two polarities. Not good and evil.* [83]

> *Therefore there is no evil—only the lack of knowledge.* [84]

SALVATION

The Christian view of salvation should be rejected.

[We should] surrender all the fallacious ideas of forgiveness, vicarious atonement, divine mercy and the rest of the opiates which superstition offers to the sinner. [85]

[The Jesus of the Aquarian Gospel]: I am disturbed about this service of the pascal feast. I thought the temple was the house of God where love and kindness dwell. Do you not hear the bleating of those lambs, the pleading of those doves that men are killing over there? Do you not smell that awful stench that comes from burning flesh? Can man be kind and just, and still be filled with cruelty? A God that takes delight in sacrifice, in blood and burning flesh, is not my Father-God. I want to find a God of love, and you, my master, you are wise, and surely you can tell me where to find the God of love. [86]

[Orthodox Christianity presents] a picture of the Christ impossible for the majority of thinking people today to accept — as the One and Only Son of God, sacrificed by His Loving Father to save Humanity from the results of its sins; as a Blood Sacrifice straight out of the old and outworn Jewish Dispensation. [87]

Salvation is self-earned.

Man is his own Satan just as man is his own salvation. [88]

The hypothesis of reincarnation shows our inherent divinity, and the method by which the latent becomes actual. Instead of the ignoble belief that we can fling our sins upon another, it makes personal responsibility the keynote of life. It is the ethics of self-help. It is the moral code of self-reliance. It is the religion of self-respect. [89]

Reincarnation is a vital part of the process of salvation.

Reincarnation is like show business. You just keep doing it until you get it right. [90]

[Reincarnation] is the process which allows each soul to experience every human condition as the path back to full spirituality and eventual reuniting with the God force. [91]

The third and last of the basic postulates of The Secret Doctrine *is the fundamental identity of all souls with the universal Oversoul . . . and the obligatory pilgrimage of every soul through a cycle of incarnation.* [92]

Salvation is the realization of one's innate divinity.

God transcendent can lead one on the path of knowing. Only God realized within one's self, God immanent in other words, can lead to being from which knowing ultimately springs. [93]

On the fact of God and of man's relation to the divine, on the fact of immortality and of the continuity of divine revelation, and upon the fact of the constant emergence of Messengers from the divine center, the new world religion will be based. To these facts must be added man's assured, instinctive knowledge of the existence of the path to God and of his ability to tread it, when the evolutionary process has brought him to the point of a fresh orientation to divinity and to the acceptance of the fact of God Transcendent and of God Immanent within every form of life. [94]

Thus it is an At-one-ment, a unifying force, by which the separated lives are gradually made conscious of their unity, laboring to develop in each a self-consciousness, which shall at last know itself to be one with all others, and its root One and divine. [95]

Christ is Divine, having perfected Himself and manifested the Divinity potential in each of us. [96]

We ascend until we reach the pinnacle of that which life is spent to build—the Temple of Perfected Man. [97]

Christ (known as Lord Maitreya) said: My purpose is to show man that he need fear no more, that all of Light and Truth rests within his heart, that when this simple fact is known man will become God. [98]

Man is an emerging God and thus requires the formation of modes of loving which will allow this God to flourish. [99]

Eventually, man will come to know himself as the Divine Being he is. [100]

Peace on the outside comes from peace on the inside. Peace on the inside comes from understanding that we are all God. [101]

You each need to become masters of your own souls, which is to say, the realization of yourselves as God. [102]

If everyone was taught one basic spiritual law, your world would be a happier, healthier place. And that law is this: Everyone is God. Everyone. The greatest threat to Earth is spiritual ignorance. . . . When everyone is aligned with the knowledge that each is part of God, the consciousness of civilization will reflect peace — peace within. Recognize that within each individual is the divine cosmic truth that you term God. [103]

The total understanding and realization of my self might require eons for me to accomplish. But when that awareness is achieved, I will be aligned completely with that unseen Divine Force we call God. [104]

The New Age is essentially a time in planetary history when the fruits of revelation given and anchored by Jesus come into being. In human terms, this means it is a time when we learn to be at one with God ourselves, to be Christs ourselves. This is also the revelation of esoteric disciplines, which have always been esoteric because they dealt with the reality of man's inner divinity and how to actualize it, rather than with the forms and doctrines relating to forming relationships with an external deity or Christ. Yet orthodox Christianity has a strong mystical side that, to the best of its ability, has taught the imitation of Christ. It has not fully dared the cosmic breadth of Jesus revelation ("Ye are gods." "All that I do, you shall do, and greater.") [and] has suggested imitation of Jesus, not actually being the Christ. [105]

Lucifer and the Christ are partners in the endeavor of bringing about humankind's salvation.

> *Lucifer works within each of us to bring us to wholeness, and as we move into a new age, which is the age of man's wholeness, each of us in some way is brought to that point which I term the Luciferic initiation.* [106]

> *Lucifer, like Christ, stands at the door of man's consciousness and knocks. If man says, "Go away because I do not like what you represent, I am afraid of you," Lucifer will play tricks on that fellow. If man says, "Come in, and I will give to you the treat of my love and understanding and I will uplift you in the light and presence of the Christ, my outflow," then Lucifer becomes something else again. He becomes the being who carries that great treat, the ultimate treat, the light of wisdom.* [107]

> *Lucifer moves in to create the light within that light, that wisdom, that love into creation so what has been forged in the furnace of creation can become a light unto the world and not simply stagnate within the being.* [108]

UNIVERSALISM

> *Your world religions are on the right track basically, but they do not teach that every individual is fundamentally the creator and controller of his own destiny. They teach that God assumes such a role. What I am endeavoring to explain is that each individual is a co-creator with God.* [109]

> *The Exponents and the Representatives of all the world faiths are there waiting—under His [the Christ's] guidance—to reveal to all those who today struggle in the maelstrom of world affairs, and who seek to solve the world crisis, that they are not alone. God Transcendent is working through the Christ and the spiritual Hierarchy to bring relief.* [110]

> *There are a number of paths that can help us return to that experience of unity, that can help us feel at home again in the spiritual*

and religious states of consciousness. In Unfinished Animal *Theodore Roszak lists over 150 such paths!* [111]

God works in many ways, through many faiths and religious agencies; this is one reason for the elimination of nonessential doctrines. By the emphasizing of the essential doctrines and in their union will the fullness of truth be revealed. This the new world religion will do, and its implementation will proceed apace after the reappearance of the Christ. [112]

FUTURE EVENTS: THE REAPPEARANCE OF CHRIST

Jesus of Nazareth is not the Christ who reappears.

The Christ Who will return will not be like the Christ Who (apparently) departed. [113]

The Christ is not God. When I say, "the coming of Christ," I don't mean the coming of God, I mean the coming of a divine man, a man who has manifested His divinity by the same process that we are going through — the incarnational process, gradually perfecting Himself. [114]

Jesus (of Nazareth) now lives in a Syrian body which is some 600 years old, and has His base in Palestine. [115]

In the last 2,000 years [Jesus has] worked in the closest relation to the Christ, saving His time and energy where possible, and has special work to do with the Christian churches. He is one of the Masters Who will very shortly return to outer work in the world, taking over the Throne of St. Peter, in Rome. He will seek to transform the Christian churches, insofar as they are flexible enough to respond correctly to the new reality which the return of the Christ and the Masters will create. [116]

[The Christ who will appear] is a reincarnation of the Christ spirit in an occult master who has lived in the Himalayas for the past 2,000 years. [117]

The world will improve before Christ reappears.

That the major required preparation is a world at peace; however, that peace must be based on an educated goodwill, which will lead inevitably to right human relations, and, therefore, to the establishment (figuratively speaking) of line of light between nation and nation, religion and religion, group and group, and man and man. [118]

A measure of peace should be restored in the world. [119]

The principle of Sharing should be in process of controlling economic affairs. [120]

The energy of goodwill should be manifesting, and leading to the implementation of right human relationships. [121]

The political and religious organizations throughout the world should be releasing their followers from authoritarian supervision over their beliefs and thinking. [122]

Christ will bring global peace and unity.

He will reappear and guide mankind into a civilization and a state of consciousness in which right human relations and worldwide cooperation for the good of all will be the universal keynote. [123]

Christ will teach the world.

Certain teachings will be given and certain energies will be released by Him in the routine of His work and coming. [124]

Christ will communicate to the world telepathically.

One day soon, men and women all over the world will gather round their radio and television sets to hear and see the Christ: to see His face, and to hear His words dropping silently into their minds—in their own language. [125]

In this way they will know that He is truly the Christ, the World Teacher. . . . Also in this way, the Christ will demonstrate the future ability of the race as a whole to communicate mentally, telepathically, over vast distances and at will. [126]

Christ will set up a new world religion.

The implementation of the new world religion will proceed apace, after the reappearance of the Christ. [127]

On the fact of God and of man's relation to the divine, on the fact of immortality and of the continuity of divine revelation, and upon the fact of the constant emergence of Messengers from the divine center, the new world religion will be based. To these facts must be added man's assured, instinctive knowledge of the existence of the path to God and of his ability to tread it, when the evolutionary process has brought him to the point of a fresh orientation to divinity and to the acceptance of the fact of God Transcendent and of God Immanent within every form of life. These are the foundational truths upon which the world religion of the future will rest. [128]

Christ will set up a new economic system.

[This will] involve the reconstruction of the world financial and economic order. [129]

[By his] presence in the world, He seeks to save millions from death and misery through starvation, and to release from bondage those now languishing in the prisons of the world for the "crime" of independent thought. [130]

Christ will set up a new government.

World government will not be imposed on mankind but will be the result of the manifested brotherhood. The sharing and co-operation of all mankind, the redistribution of the produce of the world, will result in world government. Any attempt to achieve or

*impose world government without the acceptance of sharing is
doomed to failure.*[131]

Christ has reappeared.

Christ said he would reappear in June 1945.[132]

*He [Christ] came into the world by aeroplane and so fulfilled the
prophecy of "coming in the clouds." On July 8, 1977 He descended from the Himalayas into the Indian subcontinent and went
to one of the chief cities there. He had an acclimatization period
between July 8 and 18, and then on July 19 entered a certain modern country by aeroplane. He is now an ordinary man in the
world—an extraordinary, ordinary man.*[133]

*He is today and has been actively working—through the medium
of the spiritual Hierarchy of our planet, of which He is the
"Head"—for the welfare of humanity.*[134]

The New Age is already here.

*A number of prophecies have been given relative to forthcoming
destruction and world change through cataclysm. Are we to expect this? Are we to expect a nuclear war, for example, to cleanse
the Earth? What can we do to promote the consciousness of the
New Age? This revelation came in answer to these questions. Basically, it can be summed up by saying that the New Age is here
now. It has taken shape and taken form.*[135]

Notes

1. Shirley MacLaine, *Out on a Limb* (New York: Bantam, 1983), 148.
2. Ibid., 203.
3. Ibid., 207.
4. Ibid., 335.
5. Shirley MacLaine, *Dancing in the Light* (New York: Bantam, 1985), 113.
6. Ibid., 120.
7. Ibid., 328.
8. Alice Bailey, *The Reappearance of the Christ* (New York: Lucis, 1979), 126.

9. Levi, *The Aquarian Gospel of Jesus the Christ* (Marina del Rey, Calif.: DeVorss, 1982), 15.
10. Ibid., 15.
11. Ibid., 16.
12. Benjamin Creme, *The Reappearance of the Christ and the Masters of Wisdom* (North Hollywood, Calif.: Tara Center, 1980), 108.
13. David Spangler, *Reflections of the Christ* (Findhorn, Scotland: Findhorn, 1978), 77.
14. David Spangler, *Revelation: The Birth of the New Age* (San Francisco: Rainbow Bridge, 1976), 19.
15. Ibid., 21.
16. Ibid., 22.
17. Ibid., 23-24.
18. Ibid., 77.
19. Bailey, *Reappearance of the Christ,* 147.
20. Levi, *The Aquarian Gospel,* 17.
21. Spangler, *Reflections of the Christ,* 87.
22. Ibid. 29.
23. Creme, *Reappearance of the Christ,* 115.
24. Spangler, *Revelation,* 60.
25. Creme, *Reappearance of the Christ,* 134.
26. MacLaine, *Out on a Limb,* 204.
27. Ibid., 326.
28. Spangler, *Revelation,* 60.
29. Creme, *Reappearance of the Christ,* 44.
30. Max Heindel, *Blavatsky and the Secret Doctrine* (1933 reprint) (Marina del Rey, Calif.: DeVorss, 1979), 61-64.
31. G. de Purucker, *Studies in Occult Philosophy,* (Pasadena, Calif.: Theosophical University Press, 1973), 356.
32. Spangler, *Reflections of the Christ,* 82.
33. Bailey, *Reappearance of the Christ,* 147.
34. Creme, *Reappearance of the Christ,* 122.
35. Spangler, *Revelation,* 221.
36. Levi, *The Aquarian Gospel,* 240-241.
37. Creme, *Reappearance of the Christ,* 28.
38. Annie Besant, *Esoteric Christianity* (Wheaton, Ill.: Theosophical Publishing House, 1953), 96.
39. Levi, *The Aquarian Gospel,* 261.
40. Alice Bailey, *The Externalization of the Hierarchy* (New York: Lucis, 1957), 592.
41. Annie Besant, *Is Theosophy Anti-Christian?* (London: Theosophical Pub. Society, 1901), 16.
42. Creme, *Reappearance of the Christ,* 120.
43. MacLaine, *Out on a Limb,* 91.
44. Benjamin Creme, *Messages from Maitreya the Christ,* vol. 1, no. 19 (Los Angeles: Tara, 1980), 46.
45. Levi, *The Aquarian Gospel,* 36.
46. Ibid., 261.

47. Creme, *Reappearance of the Christ,* 115.
48. Spangler, *Reflections of the Christ,* 40.
49. Levi, *The Aquarian Gospel,* 15.
50. Ibid., 15.
51. George Trevelyan, *A Vision of the Aquarian Age: The Emerging Spiritual Worldview* (Walpole, N.H.: Stillpoint, 1984), 11.
52. Levi, *The Aquarian Gospel,* 57.
53. MacLaine, *Out on a Limb,* 325.
54. Ibid., 286.
55. Creme, *Reappearance of the Christ,* 44.
56. Bailey, *Externalization,* 592.
57. Besant, *Is Theosophy Anti-Christian?* 16.
58. Levi, *The Aquarian Gospel,* 255.
59. Ibid., 15.
60. Bailey, *Externalization,* 604.
61. Levi, *The Aquarian Gospel,* 263.
62. Creme, *Reappearance of the Christ,* 135-136.
63. MacLaine, *Out on a Limb,* 208.
64. Ibid., 209.
65. MacLaine, *Dancing in the Light,* 111.
66. Ibid., 124-125.
67. Ibid., 133.
68. Ibid., 257.
69. Ibid., 298.
70. Ibid., 354.
71. Ibid., 358.
72. Mark Satin, *New Age Politics,* rev. ed. (New York: Dell, 1979), 98.
73. Spangler, *Revelation,* 13.
74. MacLaine, *Dancing in the Light,* 357.
75. Spangler, *Revelation,* 38.
76. Levi, *The Aquarian Gospel,* 78.
77. MacLaine, *Dancing in the Light,* 209.
78. Ibid., 256.
79. Ibid., 360.
80. MacLaine, *Out on a Limb,* 235.
81. MacLaine, *Dancing in the Light,* 313.
82. MacLaine, *Out on a Limb,* 347.
83. MacLaine, *Dancing in the Light,* 257.
84. Ibid., 259.
85. Annie Besant, *Karma* (London: Theosophical Pub. Society, 1904), 23.
86. Levi, *The Aquarian Gospel,* 52.
87. Creme, *Reappearance of the Christ,* 25.
88. Spangler, *Reflections of the Christ,* 39.
89. L. W. Rogers, *Elementary Theosophy* (Wheaton, Ill.: Theosophical, 1956), 206.
90. MacLaine, *Out on a Limb,* 233.
91. MacLaine, *Dancing in the Light,* 355.

92. Heindel, *Blavatsky and the Secret Doctrine*, 61-64.
93. Spangler, *Reflections of the Christ*, 26.
94. Creme, *Reappearance of the Christ*, 150.
95. Besant, *Esoteric Christianity*, 143.
96. Creme, *Reappearance of the Christ*, 25.
97. Levi, *The Aquarian Gospel*, 55.
98. Creme, *Messages from Maitreya*, 98:204.
99. Ibid., 81:170.
100. Creme, *Reappearance of the Christ*, 36.
101. MacLaine, *Dancing in the Light*, 355.
102. Ibid., 356.
103. Ibid., 412.
104. Ibid., 420.
105. Spangler, *Reflections of the Christ*, 29.
106. Ibid., 44.
107. Ibid., 41.
108. Ibid., 40.
109. MacLaine, *Out on a Limb*, 198.
110. Bailey, *Externalization*, 593.
111. Satin, *Politics*, 112.
112. Bailey, *Reappearance of the Christ*, 59.
113. Bailey, *Externalization*, 612.
114. Creme, *Reappearance of the Christ*, 115.
115. Ibid., 46.
116. Ibid., 46.
117. Ibid., 54.
118. Bailey, *Reappearance of the Christ*, 14-15.
119. Creme, *Reappearance of the Christ*, 32.
120. Ibid., 32.
121. Ibid., 32.
122. Ibid., 32.
123. Bailey, *Reappearance of the Christ*, 13.
124. Ibid., 66.
125. Creme, *Reappearance of the Christ*, 37.
126. Bailey, *Reappearance of the Christ*, 37.
127. Ibid., 59.
128. Creme, *Reappearance of the Christ*, 150.
129. Ibid., 34.
130. Ibid., 37.
131. Ibid., 169.
132. Ibid., 32.
133. Ibid., 55.
134. Bailey, *Reappearance of the Christ*, 66.
135. Spangler, *Revelation*, 78-79.

APPENDIX TWO
CHRISTIAN AND NEW AGE WORLDVIEWS

	CHRISTIAN WORLDVIEW	NEW AGE WORLDVIEW
GOD	One infinite, personal Being	One potentially (or actually) infinite impersonal (or personal) Being* Present as (or in) everything
WORLD	Created out of nothing Temporal, finite	Emanated out of God Eternal
GOD-WORLD RELATION	Creator and creation are different and distinct	Creator and creation are the same
MAN'S NATURE	Soul-body unity	Soul-body duality Body mortal, soul immortal
MAN'S IMMORTALITY	Resurrection of the body	Reincarnation into another body
MAN'S ULTIMATE DESTINY	Fellowship with God	Merge with God

	CHRISTIAN WORLDVIEW	NEW AGE WORLDVIEW
MAN'S PROBLEM	Sin against holy God	Ignorance of innate divinity
SOLUTION TO MAN'S PROBLEM	Trust in the sacrifical work of Jesus Christ	Become conscious of one's innate divinity
JESUS CHRIST	The Christ	Merely a man Bearer of the Christ spirit
ATONEMENT	Jesus' death on the cross provides deliverance from sin	No real atonement Death on the cross as example of man perfectly united with God
SALVATION	By grace alone, through faith	By self-effort (enlightenment)
SOURCES OF EVIL	Free choice in this life	Free choices in past lives
END OF EVIL	Will be defeated by God	Will be reabsorbed into God, eliminating distinction between good and evil
BASIS OF ETHICS	Grounded in God	Grounded in lower manifestations of God
NATURE OF ETHICS	Absolute	Relative
LAST THINGS	God-appointed end inaugurated when Christ reigns on earth as king	Human-realized end inaugurated when humankind realizes its inherent divinity

* As seen in Appendix 1, New Agers are very inconsistent in their view as to whether God is personal or impersonal.

APPENDIX THREE
CHRISTIAN AND NEW AGE VIEWS OF MEDITATION

	CHRISTIAN	NEW AGE
OBJECT	Something (God)	Nothing (void)
PURPOSE	Worship of God	Merge with God
MEANS	Divine relevation	Human intuition
SPHERE	Through reason	Beyond reason
POWER	God's grace	Human effort
EXPERIENCE	Objective reality	Purely subjective
IMMEDIATE STATE	Concentration	Relaxation

APPENDIX FOUR
NEW AGE ETHICS

New Age writers like Mark Satin speak of such ethical principles as *developing one's self, working with Nature, being self-reliant,* and *promoting nonviolence.* These translate, he says, into such social values as *enoughness, stewardship, autonomy and community, diversity, multidimensionality, desireless love, reverence for life, species modesty,* and *quality of life.*[1]

However, none of these guidelines is absolute. Ultimately there is no difference between good and evil. As Zen Buddhist Alan Watts noted, "The notions of right and wrong and the praise and blame of others do not disturb him."[2] Just as in *Star Wars,* the Force has two sides, a good side and an evil side. Luke Skywalker tapped into the good side for pragmatic reasons, not because it was inherently *right* to tap into the good side. Love, for New Agers, is something like the Force in that it is basically neither good nor evil. By love they do not mean a voluntary act of compassion for another individual. Rather, according to Benjamin Creme, "love" is a "totally impersonal but all-inclusive cohesive, binding force which draws all men and all things together, and holds them together." It is the cohesive force of the cosmos that holds even opposites together, such as good and evil. "It is the energy which makes humanity One."[3] Mark Satin declared, "In a spiritual [i.e., mystical] state, morality is impossible." Because "if you wish for something for yourself, even guidelines or principles, you've already separated yourself out from the One."[4] Only on a lower level are there distinctions between good and evil. But on this level there are no absolutes, only voluntary and expedient rules. As Alan Watts notes, they do "not share the Western view that there is a moral law enjoined by God or by nature, which it is man's duty to obey." Rather, there are only "voluntarily assumed rules of expediency, the intent of which is to remove the hindrances to clarity of awareness."[5] New Age evangelist Shirley MacLaine stated the heart of their ethic clearly: "We are not under the law of God. We are as the law of God. We are God." She adds, "We have to totally accept ourselves—to accept the laws of self which are divine. Then we become God."[6] Thus, "Until mankind realizes there is, in truth, no good, and there is, in truth, no evil, there will be no peace."[7]

Even though ultimately there is no good or evil, still, not everything in this world is equally good. For example, most New Agers favor abortion as a punishment for the baby's bad karma. Many favor homosexuality as an inevitable result of decisions made in a previous life. A person may have, for example, a female soul from a previous life and a male body from this life. How then, do we decide what is right and what is wrong? We should simply do what we *feel* is right. Shirley MacLaine says, "They [her spiritual guides] told me to trust my feelings."[8] In a candid passage, she writes, "Let your mind go. Don't let the left brain judge what you are thinking. Give your right brain more space. As a matter of fact, don't think."[9]

The difference between a Christian and a New Age ethic can be summarized as follows in the chart shown on page 139.

In a Christian ethic, God values each individual because he is made in His image (Gen. 1:27, 9:6). A New Age ethic, by contrast, stresses the group over the individual. Alice Bailey revealed how the individual would be subordinated to the whole when she wrote, "In the coming world state, the individual citizen gladly and deliberately and with full consciousness of all that he is doing will subordinate his personality to the good of the whole."[10]

There is also a marked difference between a Christian and a New Age view of the use of force by a government, particularly in war. New Agers believe that when we all realize that we are God, then we will stop fighting each other. War results from ignorance—ignorance of our own divinity. By marked contrast, Christians believe that humans are evil (Rom. 3:10) and that war results from their evil desires and greed (James 4:1-2). Thus, as Francis Schaeffer noted, "In a fallen world, force in some form will always be necessary."[11] So while war is undesirable, nevertheless, because men are sinful, war is sometimes unavoidable.[12]

	CHRISTIAN	NEW AGE
SOURCE OF ETHIC	God	Man
NATURE OF ETHIC	Absolute	Relative
FOCUS OF ETHIC	Charity (Love)	Whole
AIM OF ETHIC	Individuals	Unity
VIEW OF GOOD AND EVIL	Opposites	Same
VIEW OF SIN	Real	Illusory
VIEW OF MAN	Sinful	Good
HOW RIGHTEOUS-NESS IS ACHIEVED	By God's grace	By human effort
VIEW OF THE USE OF FORCE	Necessary	Harmful

Notes

1. Mark Satin, *New Age Politics,* rev. ed. (New York: Dell, 1979), 103-108.
2. Alan Watts, *The Way of Zen* (New York: Random House, 1974), 20.
3. Benjamin Creme, *The Reappearance of the Christ and the Masters of Wisdom* (North Hollywood, Calif.: Tara Center, 1980), 123.
4. Satin, *New Age Politics,* 98.
5. Watts, *The Way of Zen,* 52.
6. Shirley MacLaine, *Dancing in the Light* (New York: Bantam, 1985), 247.
7. Ibid., 342.
8. Shirley MacLaine, *Out on a Limb* (New York: Bantam, 1983), 210.
9. MacLaine, *Dancing in the Light,* 312.
10. Alice Bailey, *Education in the New Age* (New York: Lucis, 1954), 122.
11. Francis Schaeffer, *A Christian Manifesto* (Westchester, Ill.: Crossway, 1981), 107.
12. Some New Agers (e.g., Benjamin Creme) seem to advocate the eradication of orthodox monotheists (Christians, Jews, and Muslims) because they hinder the progress of the New Age movement.

APPENDIX FIVE
TEN WARNING SIGNS OF THE NEW AGE MOVEMENT

Not every New Age institution, religious organization, service, and product will come with a New Age label stamped for public view. How, then, can we guard ourselves from a movement which is often subtly couched in popular culture? Below are ten warning signs that should alert you to a possible New Age worldview.

1. Names
The New Age movement comes under many different names—the Aquarian Conspiracy, New Consciousness, New Orientalism, Cosmic Humanism, Cosmic Consciousness, Mystical Humanism, Human Potential Movement, Holistic Health Movement, to name a few.

2. Buzz Words
Favorite words used by New Agers include *awakening, centering, consciousness, cosmic energy, enlightenment, force of life, global village, holistic, human potential, networking, planetary vision, spaceship earth, synergistic, transcendental, transformational,* and *transpersonal.* Not everyone who uses these words is a New Age advocate, of course. But the frequent New Age use of these words and related words should alert us to the possibility of an underlying New Age worldview.

3. Symbols
New Age symbols include the rainbow, pyramid, triangle, eye in a triangle, Pegasus (the winged horse from Greek mythology), concentric circles, rays of light, swastika, *yin* and *yang* (the familiar Oriental symbol of light and dark contained in a circle), and unicorn. Again, the use

of these symbols does not necessarily indicate New Age connections, just as wearing a cross does not mean the person is a Christian. It is unfortunate that such lovely (and, at one time, *Christian*) symbols as the rainbow and the unicorn are now used so often by New Agers. Crystals — sold in many sizes and colors at many kinds of stores — are probably the most familiar symbols of the New Age movement.

It is not always easy to draw the line between New Age beliefs and occult beliefs, and, indeed, the two overlap in many ways. Thus many symbols of the occult — the goat's head and the pentagram, for example — are also used by New Agers.

4. Impersonal Force or Ever-Changing God
If God is spoken of in terms of either an impersonal Being (identified with the world or energy in any way) or as a potentially infinite, ever-changing God, then you have probably stumbled upon New Age ground. Sad to say, many so-called Christians, including many respected pastors, speak of God in this way.

5. Human Potential
Be alert as to how many movies, songs, lectures, literature, and even business seminars claim that humans possess "unlimited potential." Carried to its logical conclusion, this is just another way of saying that we are divine.

6. Human Goodness
New Age thought is essentially a form of humanism. New Agers carry the humanistic belief in the essential goodness of man to the point of godhood. Be careful of any teaching that emphasizes the goodness of man or ignores the reality of sin in the world.

7. Sorcery
When seminars and books speak of human potential, be attentive for modernized forms of sorcery. Sorcery may be defined as the attempt to manipulate objects, people, or events by one's will or mind. "Visualizing" or "imaging" an event that one wishes to occur is essentially an occult practice. (This does not mean, of course, that praying and hoping something will occur is necessarily sorcery.)

8. Christ-Consciousness
We should be particularly wary when someone refers to Jesus Christ as "the Christ spirit" or "Christ-consciousness." Generally, when New Agers (and many liberal Christians) speak of Christ, they are not referring to the historical Jesus spoken of in the New Testament and the great Christian creeds. If they do speak of the historical Jesus, they usually refer to Him as only one of several Christ figures in human history.

9. Mystical Feeling

New Age thought emphasizes using feelings to determine truth. Shirley MacLaine admitted that she had no proof for reincarnation, but she *felt* it was true. Mysticism is appealing to those who want to ignore their rational faculties. The New Agers would have us put logic aside, while the God of the Bible encourages us to love Him with all our heart, soul, and *mind* (Matt. 22:37-38).

10. World Unity

The New Age movement believes in the unity of all religions and the eventual cooperation of all governments. Thus New Agers are a strong force behind both the world peace and the ecumenical movements.

If we discover any one of these warning signs in a movie, TV program, book, song, or lecture, then our "spiritual detectors" should be on the alert for possible New Age influence. As with the warning signals of cancer, no one symptom is ever a sure sign that the disease is present.

GLOSSARY

Brahman. In Hinduism, the principal and ultimate reality, which is identical with all that is. (See also **Pantheism.**)

Christ-consciousness. The state of being aware, as many great religious leaders supposedly were, that you are Christ, or that you are God.

Enlightenment. The realization that you are God (akin to self-actualization).

Hypnotic regression. The process by which one is said to recall past-life memories through hypnosis.

Inner healing. The practice that aims to heal our internal, immaterial aspects through prayer, resolving past conflict and visualizing the presence of Jesus.

Karma. The law of cause and effect, which says that for every action in this life there is a reaction in the next life. That is, what we sow in this life we will reap in a future incarnation.

Lord Maitreya. The New Age Christ, who is said to be the fulfillment of all the great religious leaders of the world. Maitreya was originally a savior in Buddhist thought.

New Age movement. A loosely knit group of individuals and organizations that fundamentally believe that persons will all evolve into God and achieve a global unity that will transcend religious, racial, cultural, and political ideologies.

Panentheism. The belief that although God is potentially infinite, he is actually finite. Also, the belief that God includes the world as part, but not the whole of His being.

Pantheism. The belief that God is identical with all that exists. All is God and God is all, and there is no difference between God and the world.

Reincarnation. The belief that the soul after death passes into another body.

Self-actualization. The state of fulfilling one's potential so fully that one realizes one's self-deity.

Theism. Belief in God. More specifically, the belief that God is the cause and sustainer of the world. God and the world are not regarded as identical. God is beyond the world, yet also active in it.

Transchannelers. People who claim to help us communicate with the spirit world by becoming "human telephones."

Visualization. Attempts to manipulate reality through the mind.

BIBLIOGRAPHY

Books by New Age Authors

Bailey, Alice. *The Externalization of the Hierarchy.* New York: Lucis, 1957.

———. *The Reappearance of the Christ.* New York: Lucis, 1979.

Besant, Annie. *Esoteric Christianity.* Wheaton, Ill.: Theosophical Publishing House, 1953.

———. *Is Theosophy Anti-Christian?* London: Theosophical Publishing Society, 1901.

———. *Karma.* London: Theosophical Publishing Society, 1904.

Creme, Benjamin. *Messages from Maitreya the Christ.* Vol 1., No. 19. Los Angeles: Tara, 1980.

———. *The Reappearance of the Christ and the Masters of Wisdom.* North Hollywood, Calif.: Tara Center, 1980.

Ferguson, Marilyn. *The Aquarian Conspiracy: Personal and Social Transformation in the 1980s.* Los Angeles: J. P. Tarcher, 1980. (A 1987 edition of the book contains some new material.)

Heindel, Max. *Blavatsky and the Secret Doctrine.* 1933. Reprint. Marina del Rey, Calif.: DeVorss, 1979.

Levi. *The Aquarian Gospel of Jesus the Christ.* 1907. Reprint. Marina del Rey, Calif.: DeVorss, 1982.

MacLaine, Shirley. *Dancing in the Light.* New York: Bantam, 1985.

———. *It's All in the Playing.* New York: Bantam, 1987.

———. *Out on a Limb.* New York: Bantam, 1983.

Rogers, L. W. *Elementary Theosophy.* Wheaton, Ill.: Theosophical Publishing House, 1956.

Satin, Mark. *New Age Politics.* Rev. ed. New York: Dell, 1979.

Spangler, David. *Reflections of the Christ.* Findhorn, Scotland: Findhorn, 1978.

———. *Revelation: The Birth of the New Age.* San Francisco: Rainbow Bridge, 1976.

Trevelyan, George. *A Vision of the Aquarian Age: The Emerging Spiritual World View.* Walpole, N.H.: Stillpoint, 1984.

Magazines:

East-West Journal, New Age Journal, New Realities, Whole Life Times, and *Yoga Journal.*

Books by Critics of the New Age Movement

Bowen, William, Jr. *Globalism: America's Demise.* Shreveport, La.: Huntington House, 1984.

Clark, David K. *The Pantheism of Alan Watts.* Downers Grove, Ill.: InterVarsity, 1978.

Crouse, Bill. *A Primer on Occult Philosophy.* Dallas: Probe Insight Paper, 1983.

Cumbey, Constance E. *The Hidden Dangers of the Rainbow.* Shreveport, La.: Huntington House, 1983.

————. *A Planned Deception: The Staging of a New Age Messiah.* East Detroit, Mich.: Pointe, 1985.

Geisler, Norman L. *False Gods of Our Time.* Eugene, Oreg.: Harvest House, 1985.

Geisler, Norman L., and J. Yutaka Amano. *The Reincarnation Sensation.* Wheaton, Ill.: Tyndale House, 1986.

Geisler, Norman L., and William Watkins. *Perspectives: Understanding and Evaluating Today's Worldviews.* San Bernardino, Calif.: Here's Life, 1984.

Groothius, Douglas R. *Unmasking the New Age.* Downers Grove, Ill.: InterVarsity, 1986.

Guinness, Os. *The Dust of Death.* Downers Grove, Ill.: InterVarsity, 1973.

Hunt, Dave. *Peace, Prosperity, and the Coming Holocaust.* Eugene, Oreg.: Harvest House, 1983.

————. *Beyond Seduction: A Return to Biblical Christianity.* Eugene, Oreg.: Harvest House, 1987.

Hunt, Dave, and T. A. McMahon. *The Seduction of Christianity.* Eugene, Oreg.: Harvest House, 1985.

Johnson, David L. *A Reasoned Look at Asian Religions.* Minneapolis: Bethany House, 1985.

Maharaj, Rabindranath R. *Escape into the Light.* Eugene, Oreg.: Harvest House, 1984.

Matrisciana, Caryl. *Gods of the New Age.* Eugene, Oreg.: Harvest House, 1985.

Rasche, Carl A. *The Interruption of Eternity: Modern Gnosticism and the Origins of the New Religious Consciousness.* Chicago: Nelson-Hall, 1980.

Reisser, Paul C. *The Holistic Healers.* Downers Grove, Ill.: InterVarsity, 1983.

Rhodes, Ronald. "An Examination and Evaluation of the New Age Christology of David Spangler." Th.D. diss., Dallas Theological Seminary, 1986.

Sire, James W. *The Universe Next Door.* Downers Grove, Ill.: InterVarsity, 1976.

Vitz, Paul. *Psychology as Religion.* Grand Rapids: Eerdmans, 1977.

Wilson, Clifford, and John Weldon. *Occult Shock and Psychic Forces.* San Diego: Masters Books, 1980.

INDEX OF NAMES

149